Larry Evans

3-DIMENSIONAL MAZE ART

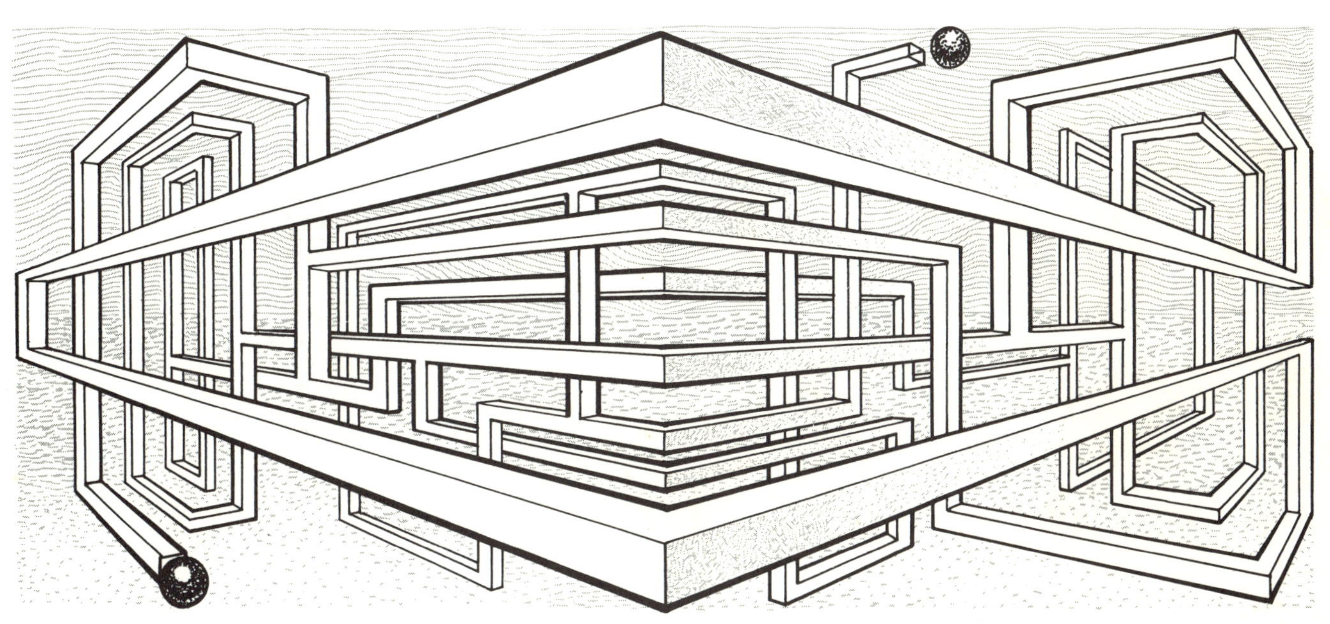

Written and Illustrated by
Larry Evans

Troubador Press San Francisco

This book is dedicated to my wife, Rosalee, who is the most beautiful, witty and intelligent woman I've ever known.

Library of Congress Cataloging in Publication Data
Evans, Larry, 1939-
Larry Evans 3-dimensional maze art.

1. Evans, Larry, 1939- 2. Maze puzzles — History. I. Title. II. Title: 3-dimensional maze art.
ND237.E78A4 1980 759.13 80-16987
ISBN 0-89844-012-2

FIRST EDITION

 Published in the United States of America by Troubador Press, 385 Fremont Street, San Francisco, California 94105. ISBN: 0-89844-012-2

TABLE OF CONTENTS

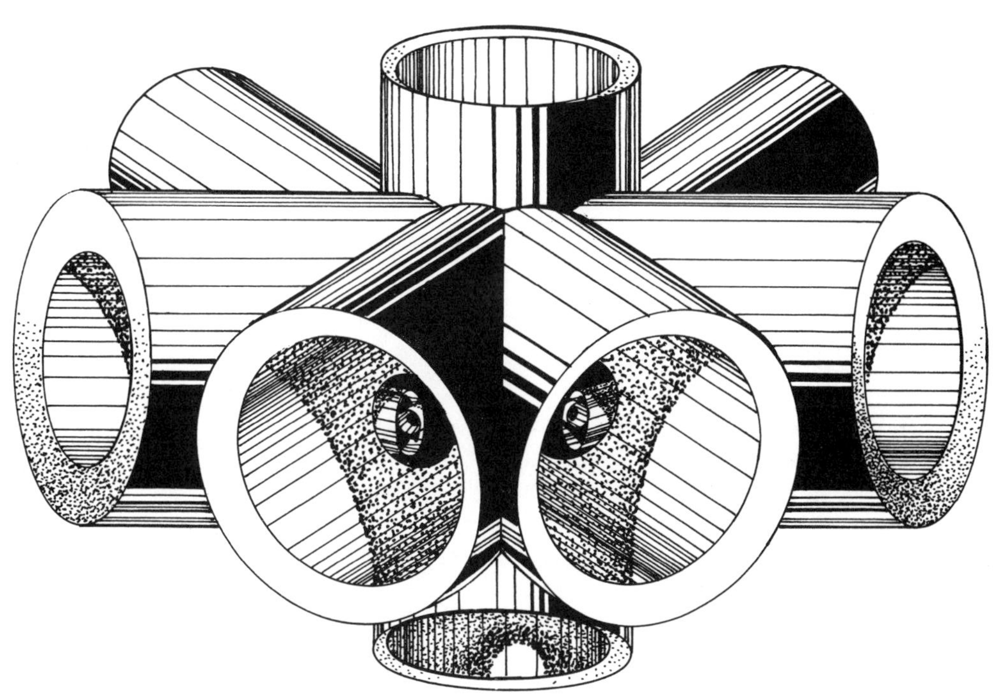

62-OB7 Right Hand 3-D Maze Connector Unit

Introduction

These three-dimensional mazes are unique. Through a canny, witty use of perspective, Larry Evans reverses the ravages of time to bring the common two-dimensional maze back to its rightful, original three-dimensional stature. Not since Theseus conquered the tortuous Cretan Labyrinth and its demonical Minotaur has this mystical puzzle form commanded such involvement.

Deftly fashioning an illusion of depth, Evans draws us *into* the maze. We cannot refuse the challenge. Through mad-house tunnels, between looming walls, around yawning voids, we prowl this sinuous symbol of life. Passageways bend, twist, clear and disappear. It isn't easy. Are we lost forever? Suddenly — the way out!

We are not lost. We have found ourselves.

Embellishing his evocative illustrations with a rich blaze of color, Evans not only heightens their three-dimensionality, but lifts them to a rank of rare graphic art. Published in prints, posters and 37 books around the world, he shares with us, for the first time in book form, his full color maze art as well as some of the secrets embraced in their creation.

In the following pages you will be absorbed in an intriguing experience. Join the quest, enjoy the fun and relish the vivid, colorful three-dimensional maze art of Larry Evans.

Malcolm Whyte, Publisher

Cretan labyrinth — Italian engraving

Chapter 1

History of the Maze

The maze, is it a puzzle or an art form? Already an enigma before the first line is drawn, the maze is a wondrous thing, a design that pre-dates history. Surely the most renowned maze in mythology is the Cretan Labyrinth, the incredible structure designed by Daedalus. Within this ingenious building lived the Minotaur. Half man and half bull, this creature destroyed any human who became lost in the maze. Theseus entered the Labyrinth, slew the Minotaur and retraced his steps by following a thread he had unrolled on his inward journey.

The Cretan Labyrinth is important to recall for several reasons. First, the theme of the Minotaur shows up in a maze design throughout the Roman era and into the Middle Ages. Greek coins minted from around 400 B.C. through 67 B.C. exhibit a maze pattern, some inscribed with the head of a bull. This certainly indicates the power of the labyrinth as a strong and universally recognized graphic symbol. But the most important aspect of the Cretan Labyrinth is the fact that it was designed as a *three-dimensional* structure. The hapless souls sent into this diabolical cavern could only experience the maze from *within*, with no clue to its solution. The difference between maze patterns as we see them today, and the thought of being buried within an endless meander with no way to look over the walls, no way to develop a clue to the ultimate solution and maybe no way out at all, is obviously considerable.

As time went by, the maze as a graphic symbol became more and more two-dimensional. The Romans used the maze pattern in mosaic pavement, several examples of which still exist in Pompeii, Rome and Salzburg, Austria.

During the Middle Ages, the churches in Europe used labyrinthian designs on both floors and walls. Rheims Cathedral had a magnificent tile maze, constructed in 1240, but destroyed in 1779 by Canon Jacquemart who couldn't stand the noise made by children tracing its paths during Mass.

16th century maze design

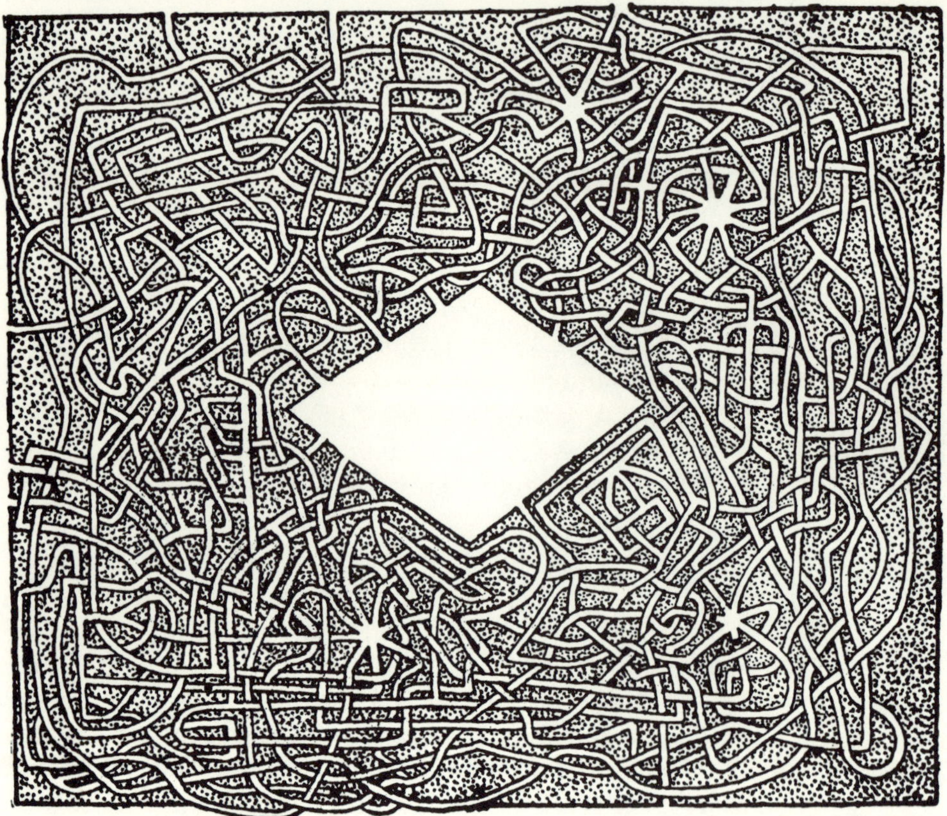

Maze design by Lewis Carroll. Travel from the center diamond over and under the pathways to the outside. This labyrinth design is an early form of three-dimensional maze.

Tile maze usage begun by the Romans set the stage for the modern two-dimensional mazes so prevalent in children's puzzles today. By reducing Daedalus' three-dimensional invention to a plan (similar to an architect's schematic drawing), a simple puzzle is achieved. An architect's plan embodies many of the same elements prevalent in two-dimensional mazes. Heavy black lines are used for walls and openings are left for doorways. In a maze, we accept the premise that the black lines are walls and try to achieve a goal by traversing the proper path.

The three-dimensional turf and hedge mazes popular in Europe in the 17th and 18th centuries were really the same as the architect's plan, as the solver could easily see his goal and the path before him.

The major difference between the Labyrinth built by Daedalus on Crete and the maze reproduced on Roman tile patterns is, of course, the illusion of depth. The way you achieve this illusion in drawing and painting is through the use of three-dimensional perspective.

What might happen if you imagined the common two-dimensional maze as an architect's plan? The complicated buildings created using schematic plans are often constructed on many levels. The mechanical tubes and electrical wiring often travel for several kilometers throughout a building. Accept the fact that the black lines of architectural plans are walls and thus two-dimensional mazes. Take it a step further and accept the premise that the paths between the walls can cross over each other. Going another step further, add the feeling of depth with the illusion of perspective.

The three-dimensional maze is the end result of projecting the Roman two-dimensional tile pattern into a field controlled by perspective. The pathways may now be pipes or tubes, but the basic concept is still the labyrinth of antiquity.

Now that you accept the illusion of perspective and see the pathway as it floats in space, take the ultimate step and project *yourself* into the puzzle. Pretend you are within the pipes and tubes. You can be an insect (p. 37) or a drop of water (p. 44) or even an electrical current or a soap bubble. Let your imagination pull you into the three-dimensional maze.

The initial question has yet to be answered. Is the maze a puzzle or an art form? To answer this question with respect to three-dimensional mazes, you must first inquire about the intentions of the artist. Does he intend for his work to be a puzzle or an art form?

A typical modern maze puzzle

Not all mazes are art. Many (see Chapter 5) are created for the express purpose of being a puzzle, with no attempt to adhere to the self-imposed restraints of fine art. The word "self-imposed" is operative here because of anarchy within the world of art. When fine art museums exhibit tree branches, sharpened at one end, as art, when a person bakes a cake and throws it at someone, and calls this "happening" art, it becomes difficult to discuss the rules of art without first defining the narrow spectrum into which this art form fits. Certainly an artist must set and then accept his own rules. The consistency of style within the boundaries he sets for himself is often a large measure of the success of the work.

The boundaries established for my three-dimensional mazes include the classic dogma of composition, color theory and perspective. Mathematical theory and visual symmetry are the basic building blocks for most mazes in this book. Aside from the rules of painting and composition there is, again, the self-imposed rule: a maze *must* work as a puzzle. The techniques of painting must remain flexible enough to allow for the puzzle to work. It is patently unfair for a viewer to spend his time involved with a maze that does not work. Puzzle creators have been pilloried for less.

This collection of three-dimensional mazes reflects a need to raise the poor, mistreated labyrinth back to its rightful place as a superior puzzle and positive art form. The decline of the maze from the historic efforts of Daedalus to the simplicity of a child's puzzle is now reversed.

"Is the maze a puzzle or an art form?" In regard to three-dimensional mazes, yes, it is both.

You are invited to see for yourself.

LARRY EVANS ·66

Chapter 2

The Metamorphosis of an Idea

The question most often asked me is, "Where do you get your ideas?" At the moment I'm writing this, I'm sitting above the Pacific Ocean on the Mendocino coast of California. Within my view is a vista of pounding surf, massive headlands and a variety of rock formations. Two giant eucalyptus trees frame the scene. The rocks and the sea form patterns that excite my interest. Caves have been eaten through the rocks and the idea of an ocean cave maze flashes before me. The trees have branches that spiral about the trunk and the idea hits me that a tree form might make a good maze. It seems that once you set a direction for yourself in the world of art, any and all experiences can, and do, lead to ideas. There goes a crow with a lizard in its beak. Maybe . . .

Ideas happen most often in an interchange of thoughts with my colleagues. A response to a pointed question often forces action destined to create new concepts, and thus ideas.

The invention of the three-dimensional maze occurred as a natural extension of my background in industrial design. Always fascinated by perspective and other forms of optical illusions, the maze form became the next logical step from my earlier experimentations with solid forms in space. *Assemblage* (p. 8) was painted several years prior to the first three-dimensional maze, but it is easy to see the roots of a solid geometric labyrinth within the boundaries of this watercolor.

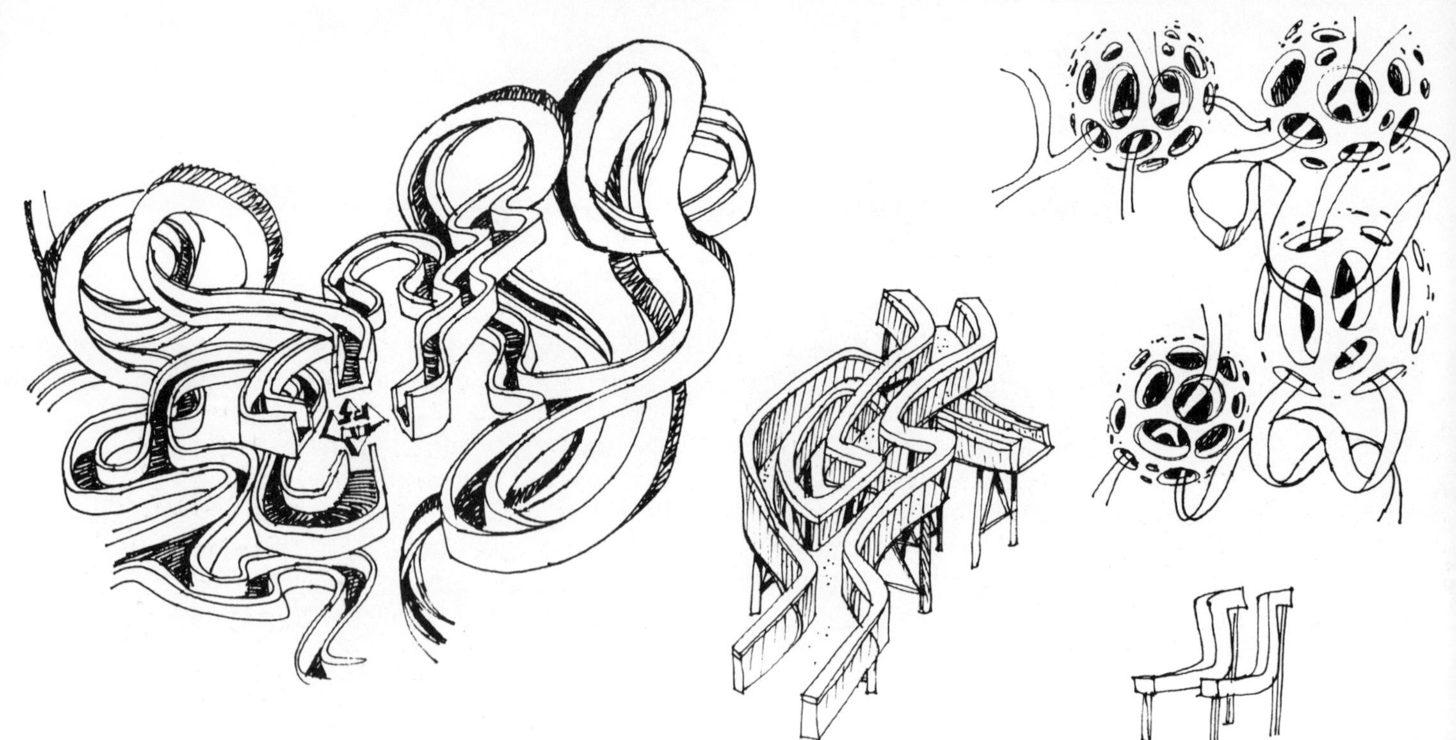

The first three-dimensional mazes were constructed on a Hawaiian vacation. They were lyrical and poetic rather than the strong graphic images that developed later. The *Bathmat Series*, shown here, was drawn on a subsequent trip where the only drawing paper available in the motel was bathmats.

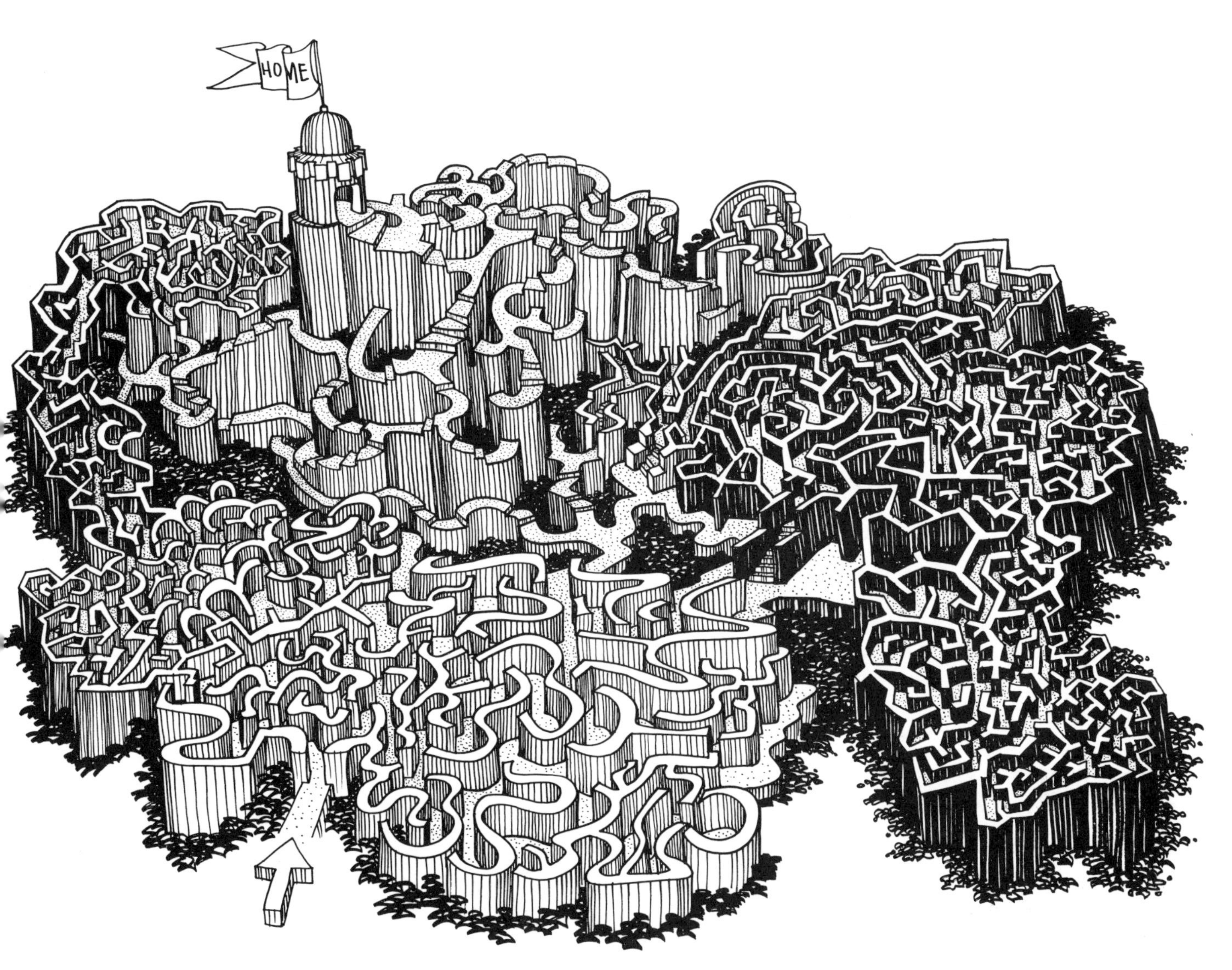

This maze is one of the earliest developmental designs. Preceding Stairs and Hollow Places (p. 13) by several months, this maze has yet to possess the true qualities of a three-dimensional maze. The walls are only an isometric projection with little actual hiding of the pathways. This composition is, however, a major advance over the Bathmat Series (p. 10), as the structure and complexity of the drawing suggest further avenues of design possibilities.

A new wrinkle is added to this unfinished project. The walls at the entry arrow have doorways within them. This simple addition totally changes the effect of the maze by circumventing the wall tops. This maze begins to exhibit many of the qualities of a true three-dimensional maze.

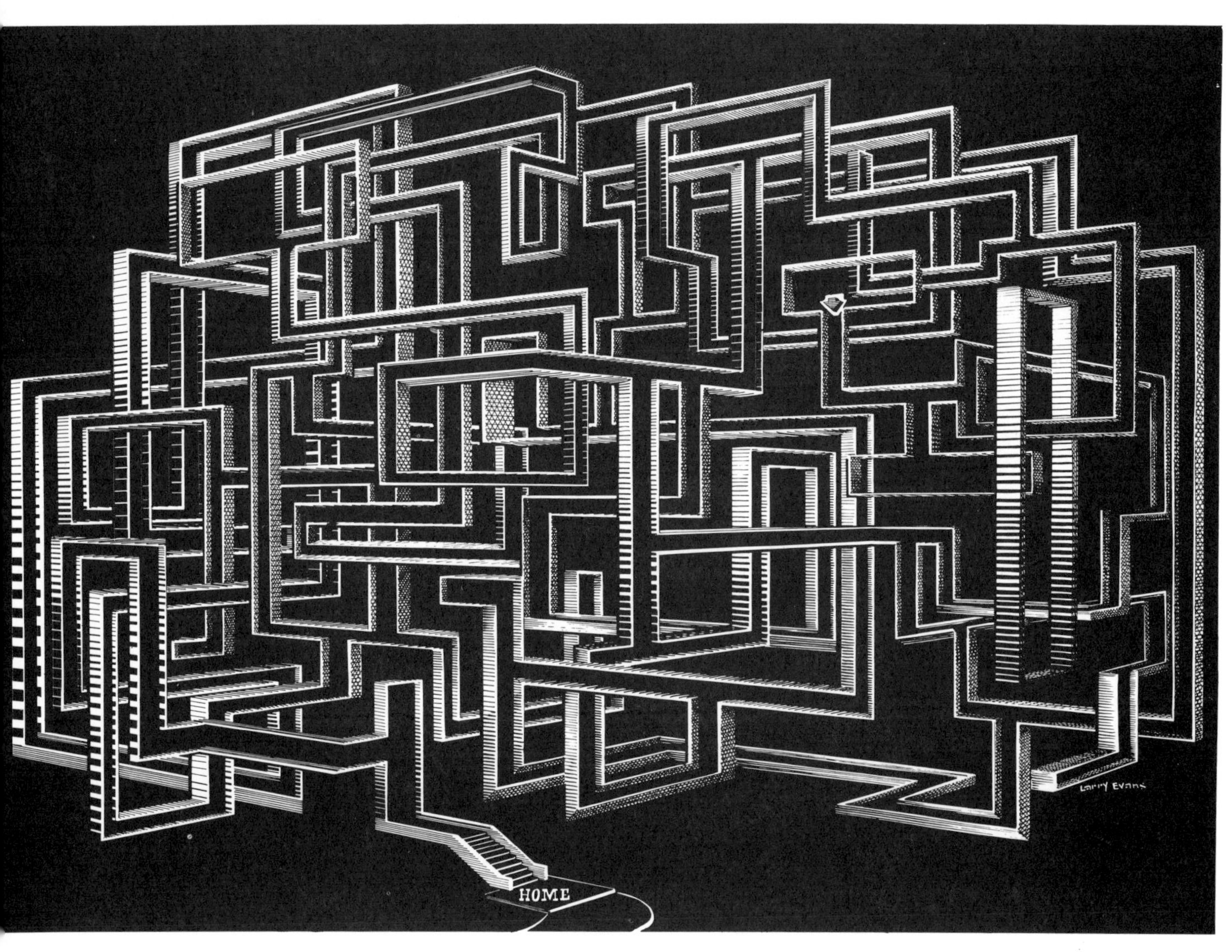

Stairs and Hollow Places (above) was the first three-dimensional maze that actually worked for me and set the direction for future work. Two years of trial and error led to the creation of this drawing and I was finally forced to realize that three-dimensional mazes would constitute a major part of my remaining years as an artist.

Upon receiving a commission to prepare six posters and a contract to create two books, three-dimensional mazes suddenly became not only a viable form of personal expression, but also a source of income. Public acceptance has been gratifying especially from young people who seem to grasp the spatial complexity more easily than their elders.

My experience with mazes has led me into the world of puzzle creation and problem solving. I find it almost impossible to restrict my energies to only one form of puzzle and that resulting research into other puzzle forms adds a depth of knowledge to the maze creations.

Chapter 3

The Three-Dimensional Maze in Construction

With the trials of invention behind me, actual construction of the mazes becomes the overriding concern. Always torn between the maze as a puzzle and the maze as an art form, a whole set of rules has to be generated:

1. The maze must have a solution; only one if possible.
2. Although controlled by the rules of perspective (or the breaking of said rules), the path must be sufficiently visible to allow the viewer to follow it.
3. New conduits and paths must be constantly searched for, regardless of the fact that, as a puzzle, one or two pathways might suffice.
4. The maze should *never* be taken so seriously that its entertaining aspects get lost (see Chapter 5).

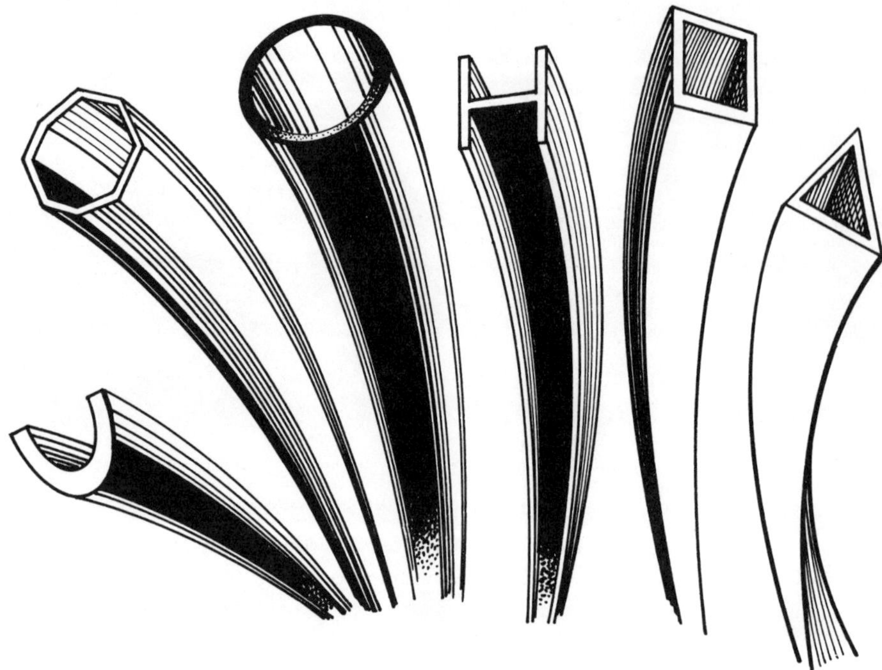

Beginning a three-dimensional maze is an exciting moment for me. No amount of planning can totally fix the design. No matter how structured the basic pattern, the paths seem to find their own relationships within the picture. The constant struggle between the puzzle and the art form creates a tension that must be controlled. It is almost impossible to begin the maze structure and not complete it at one sitting.

The desire to connect the start with the finish seems to be an almost metaphysical need. If the structure is uncompleted, the drawing seems to call me back to the board to finish it. It's like two live wires that lie only inches apart arcing across the void to complete the circuit.

Several rough sketches are first prepared to help eliminate impossible situations that might crop up halfway through the construction process. These "roughs" do not attempt to actually create a maze, but rather to develop a basic structure to follow.

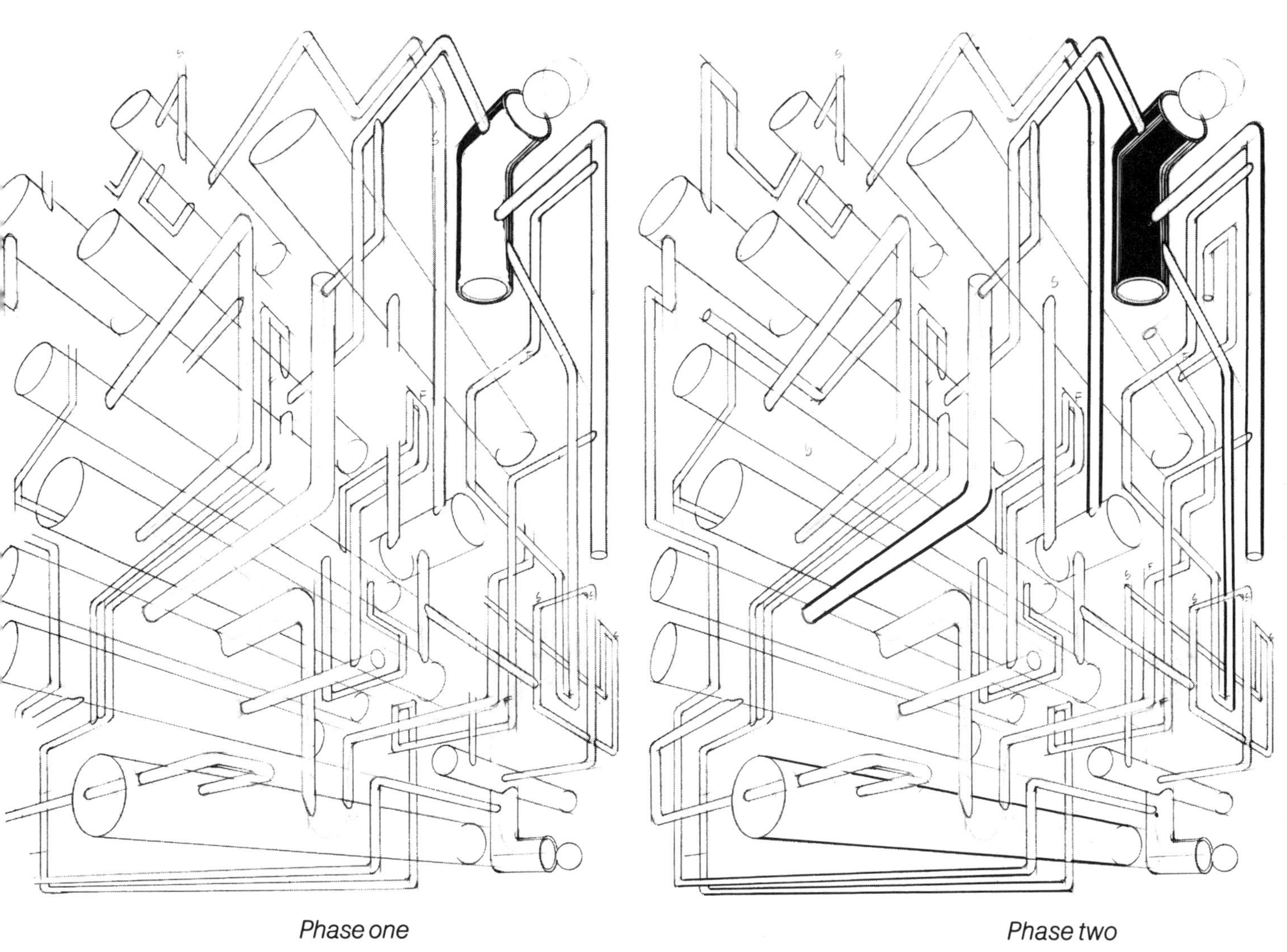

Phase one

Phase two

The infinite palette of spatial patterns makes the concept part of the maze adventure an exciting one. Polygons, interlocking polyhedra, cycloidal envelopes and hyperboloids are just a tiny selection of the possible symmetrical forms to start from. The cube alone has so many possible facets that one could spend a lifetime just exploring the various cubic relationships.

Once a basic shape (symmetrical, asymmetrical, random) and conduit (square, round, open, etc.) have been selected, the construction process begins. Both the start and finish areas are positioned and the perspective is constructed. Often, several vanishing points are used, each of which must conform to the basic shape determined in the rough sketches. The major pathways are sketched in lightly, often not connected to either the start or finish path. Equal time must be spent on developing the start direction, the finish direction, the dead ends and continuous tunnels.

The process of developing pathways continues until the basic shape is filled out and the paths have nowhere to go except to confuse the situation. There is no way to preordain just when this stage may occur in any given puzzle. After constructing several hundred mazes, you simply know when to quit.

The completed maze

Sometimes the start-finish connection is completed early on in the drawing process. Blind trails and dead ends are then the bulk of the puzzle. Every once in a while, the final stroke is the start-finish connection. As in all three-dimensional maze construction, the final solution is just as big a surprise to the builder as it is to the solver.

The completed drawing must now be tested. If you're lucky, the puzzle will work, and there *will* be a solution. Each path and turn must be tested, often using tracing paper overlays and different colored pencils. Any mistakes are now corrected and the maze proceeds to the final stage of painting or inking.

The builder/solver relationship is a special one in the world of three-dimensional mazes. The puzzle should amuse, confound, delight and stump the solver. The solver wants to defeat the puzzle, but not too easily. He *wants* to be amused, confounded and delighted, but *not* stumped. A truly successful three-dimensional maze will draw a would-be solver into its web, spin him around and send him out into the elements shaking his head in bewilderment. He'll want to plunge in again, this time looking for the hidden turn that he missed before, figuring that the builder cheated. He'll say, "Of course, there is *no* solution . . . Well, maybe a quick peek at the solution page. Oh, missed that turn a dozen times . . . ".

Tips on Solving Three-dimensional Mazes

These mazes are created with the expressed intention of stumping the would-be solver. Many people simply give up before they even try to secure a solution.

These puzzles are not easy. The additional illusion of space makes it virtually impossible to plot a path without experiencing dead ends and falling into continuous trails that lead nowhere. The reward for solving these mazes is greater than that for solving an easy puzzle. However, once you catch on to the basic concept, you will find that there is an underlying logic within the maze construction and that your participation is critical to the success of the unit as an artistic endeavor.

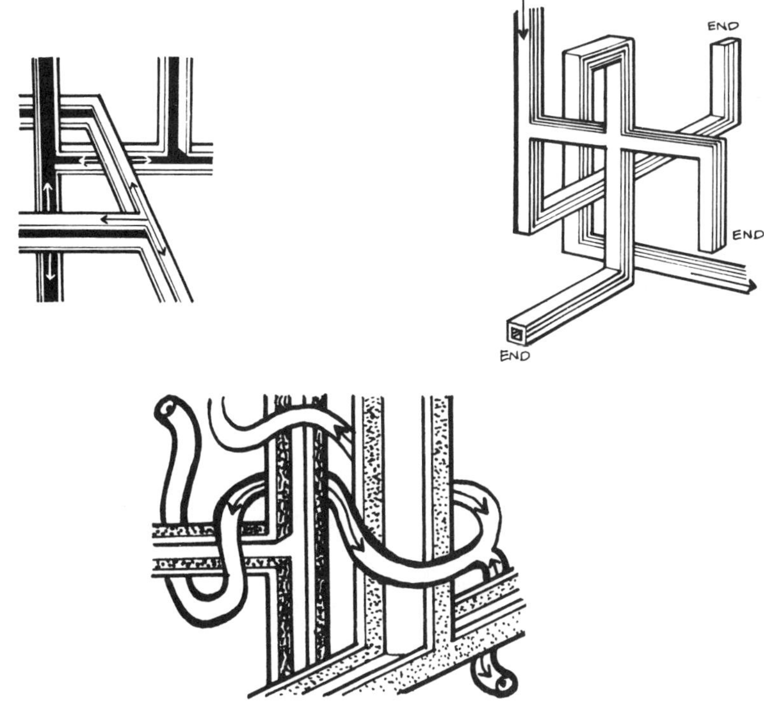

First, visually remove all the dead ends from contention, then proceed from both ends towards each other.

On the more complicated mazes, it is imperative that you envision mental road signs. Try to remember where you have been and again eliminate as much of each erroneous path as you can.

Avoid using a pencil so that the puzzles will remain fresh for the next solver. In the case of *The World's Hardest Maze* (p. 44), a light tissue overlay is recommended. Each three-dimensional maze has a solution, so don't give up! Remember, you are only blocked at the end of a path. Some paths may disappear behind other paths, but *no* path ever *ends* behind another path, or even close to one. If a tube or a conduit disappears behind another, it must reappear in a reasonable place exhibiting an obvious connection. Once you are inside a tube you must stay there. No hopping into another as they cross each other. If you wish to add a greater degree of complexity to the maze, cut a circle the size of a quarter in a piece of paper and work the puzzle as it appears through the hole.

Chapter 4

3-Dimensional Maze Gallery

This chapter contains 22 three-dimensional mazes, eight in full color. Solutions for these and all the other mazes in the book are on the last five pages. These puzzles are designed to be solved visually (without making a pencil or pen trail). You are only blocked at the end of a path and the solution comes more easily if you project yourself into the pipes and tubes. You may begin at either end of the maze, but the rule here is, never give up.

You will find that the addition of color to the three-dimensional mazes adds a special excitement to the puzzle. The interplay of hues and tonal values along with highlights and reflections bring a reality and clarity to the maze. Although many of the color plates have black as the background color, a new series of mazes is being developed using landscapes as the background. The transformation from strict uncomplicated graphic statements to compound visual compositions is a complex procedure. Constant experimentation goes on as an artist's craft blossoms and often several states evolve before the final scene is played.

Sky Pipes (p. 19)
76cm x 126cm, acrylic on canvas.
The eternal eco-system translated into a puzzle. The faucet connects with the cloud strata and eventually fills the ocean. Or, evaporation can work its magic and the puzzle reverses itself.

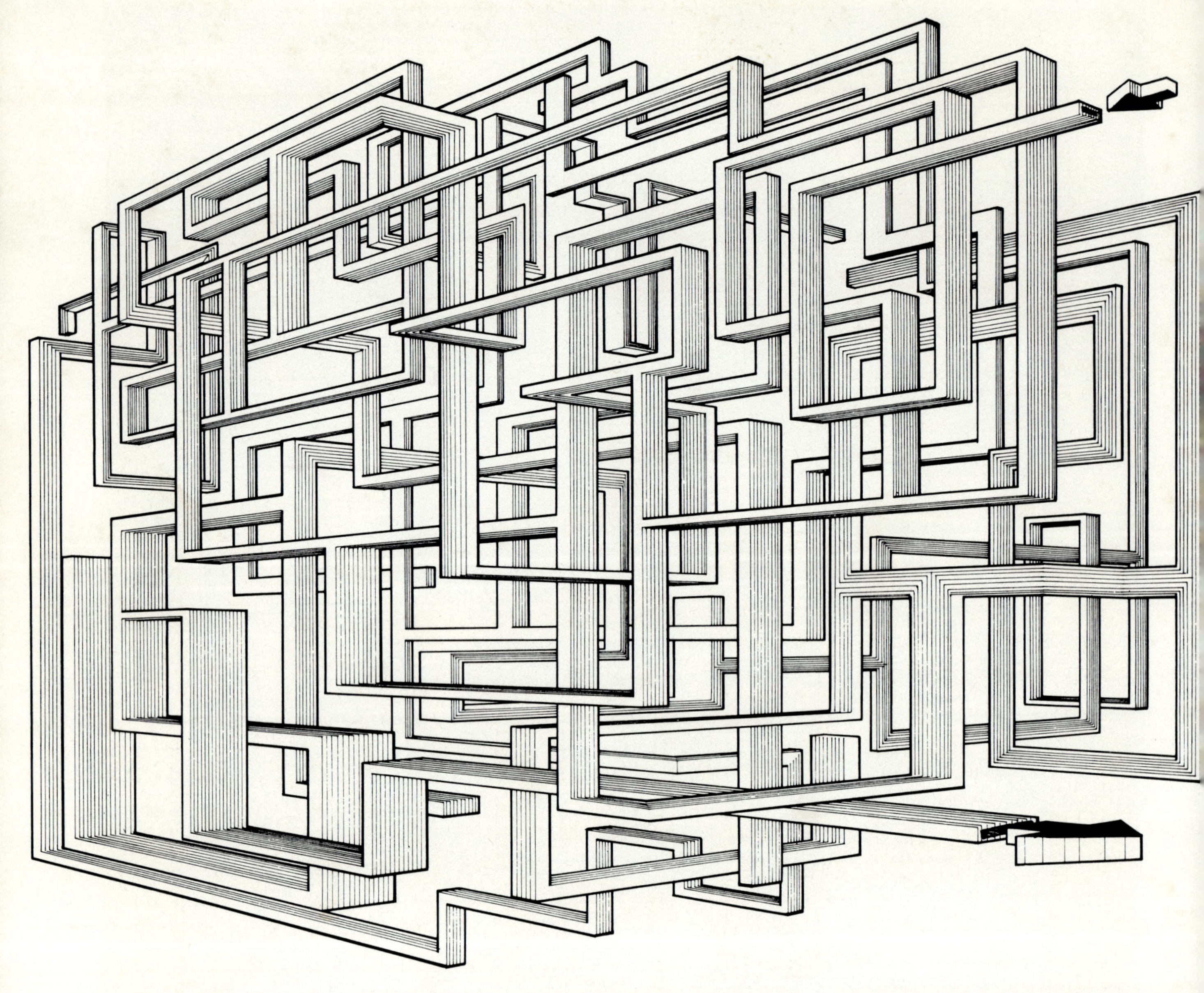

Flat Tubes
This maze has more than one solution. Remember: The paths in three-dimensional mazes cross over and under each other in perspective so you are only blocked at the end of a path.

Space Maze *(p. 21)*
76cm x 100cm, acrylic on paper.
The space traveler must traverse the time warp to connect the four outer orbs to the mother planet. Work from the center out to all four satellites or vice versa.

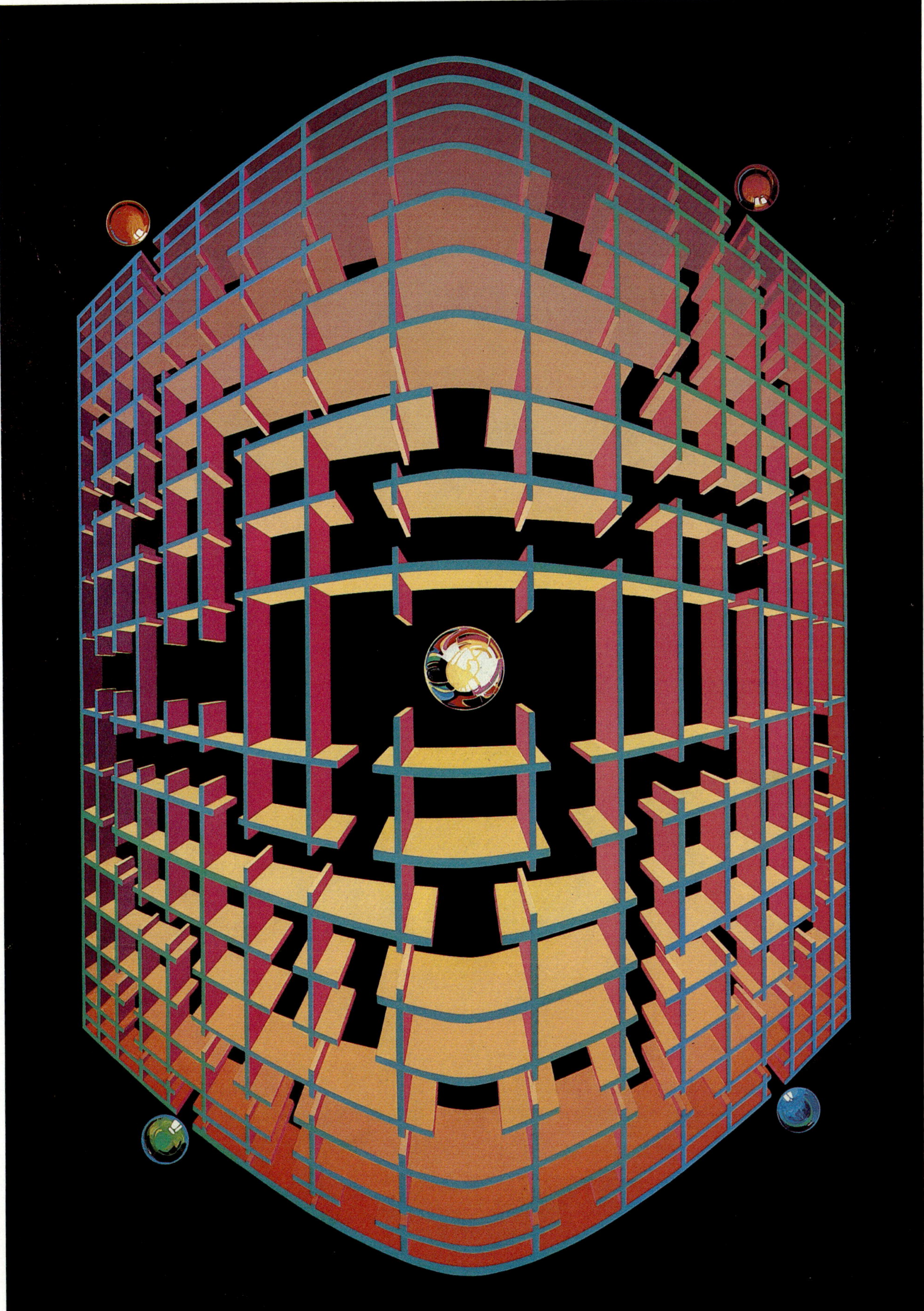

Floating Beams
First published in 3-DIMENSIONAL MAZES (Troubador Press, 1976).
Pretend you are a fly and crawl along the black path from arrow to arrow.
When the path disappears behind a wall, it keeps going. Believe me.

Inside-Out *(p. 23, top)*
50cm x 76cm, acrylic on paper.
Follow the arrows through this labyrinth from start to finish. Vanishing points on a vertical horizon line change this construction from a simple one-point perspective to a more complex composition.

Wood Pile *(p. 23, bottom)*
40cm x 56cm, mixed media
The carpenters have used their imaginations instead of the framing plan. Pretend you're a termite and stay on the proper boards to unravel this maze.

Most artists won't deal with the relationship between the work of art and the viewer. Although almost every artist wants his work to be popular, it is only rarely that the public is given an opportunity to share the artist's motivations and the message that lies buried within a given work of art. Even when a patron purchases a particular work for display within his home, all too often the choice is based on decorator requirements, not artistic communication.

The three-dimensional maze as an art form, however, tends to circumvent this communications gap. The puzzle aspect, the obvious message superimposed over the subliminal one, gives the viewer an even chance to experience a relationship with the art work and thus with the artist himself.

Steel Maze *(p. 25)*
50cm x 76cm, acrylic on paper.
The highly polished steel conduits connect into, and reflect onto, each other. This maze has been reproduced in aluminum with full color printing over the etched metal surface. A surprising result is achieved when a painting of metal is superimposed over the metal itself.

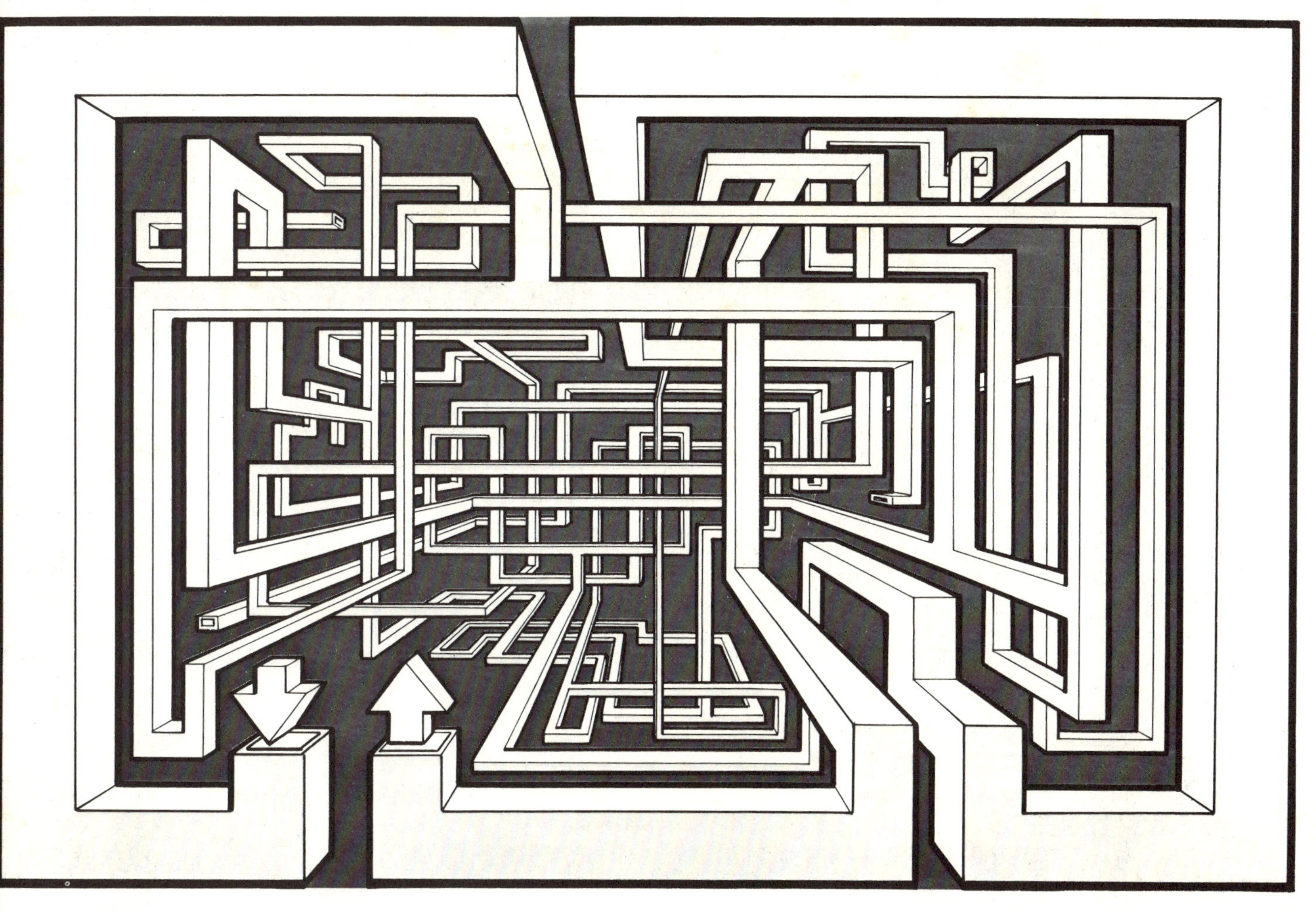

Logic Chip
This new holographic logic chip will revolutionize the computer industry, if only the input can reach the output.

Tug O' War *(p. 26)*
Follow the ropes from end to end. A dead end means you must start over but at the opposite end.

The mazes on these two pages are examples of square tubes responding to one-point perspective. The vanishing point is located directly in the center of the composition and the visual effect is similar to looking down a well or into a tunnel.

Batch Plant
Notice the similarity between this puzzle and the ancient illustration on page four. The standard two-dimensional maze is projected into the third dimension by the use of vertical walls and ellipse forms.

Four Way Maze *(p. 28)*
Each quarter panel has its own central vanishing point. The entire composition warps as the small tubes wrap in front of the larger ones.

I-Beams

This composition uses classic construction girders as the pathways. You are asked to pretend that you're a highrise construction worker and follow the beams from start to finish.

***Pipe Yard** (p. 31)*

Constructed of old and new pipes, the object of this maze is to travel through the pipes from bubble to bubble before the pipes rust through. This maze is a watercolor. Many of the color plates were first studied in watercolor before final painting.

The world of art is confusing today not only for the public, but for the artist himself as well. As traditional values change and the art world becomes more experimental, the very essence of what an artist is, or should be, gets lost in the effort to be contemporary. Working with one of the oldest art forms known to mankind, I hope to create a bridge between the public and the art itself. If the people who lived from 400 B.C. through the Middle Ages could grasp the message the maze has locked within its walls, then why not modern man with his advanced technology and sophisticated ways? The maze touches the innermost anxieties of all who dare to enter its challenge. At some time or another, we have all experienced a sense of being lost. We take the wrong road, use the wrong door or catch the wrong plane. In each case, the sense of helplessness associated with losing control takes over our consciousness. Adrenalin races through our systems and the heart beats faster. The maze is a symbol of this frustration — and its ultimate solution.

The very fact that a maze *can* be solved (although sometimes it takes a ball of thread) softens the rush of anxiety associated with being lost. As *being lost* is a primeval feeling, the emotions associated with experiencing a maze are rooted in the subconscious. When a work of art subverts the conscious blockade and passes through the outer walls of obtuse armor we all create to protect our innermost selves, a bond of basic understanding is achieved. A sense of recognition, perhaps of *deja vu*, passes through our minds. Is it possible we have been there before? Have we confronted this problem already, and were we able to solve it?

In To Out *(p. 33)*
Guide the ball inside the maze through the tubes into the pathways and out.

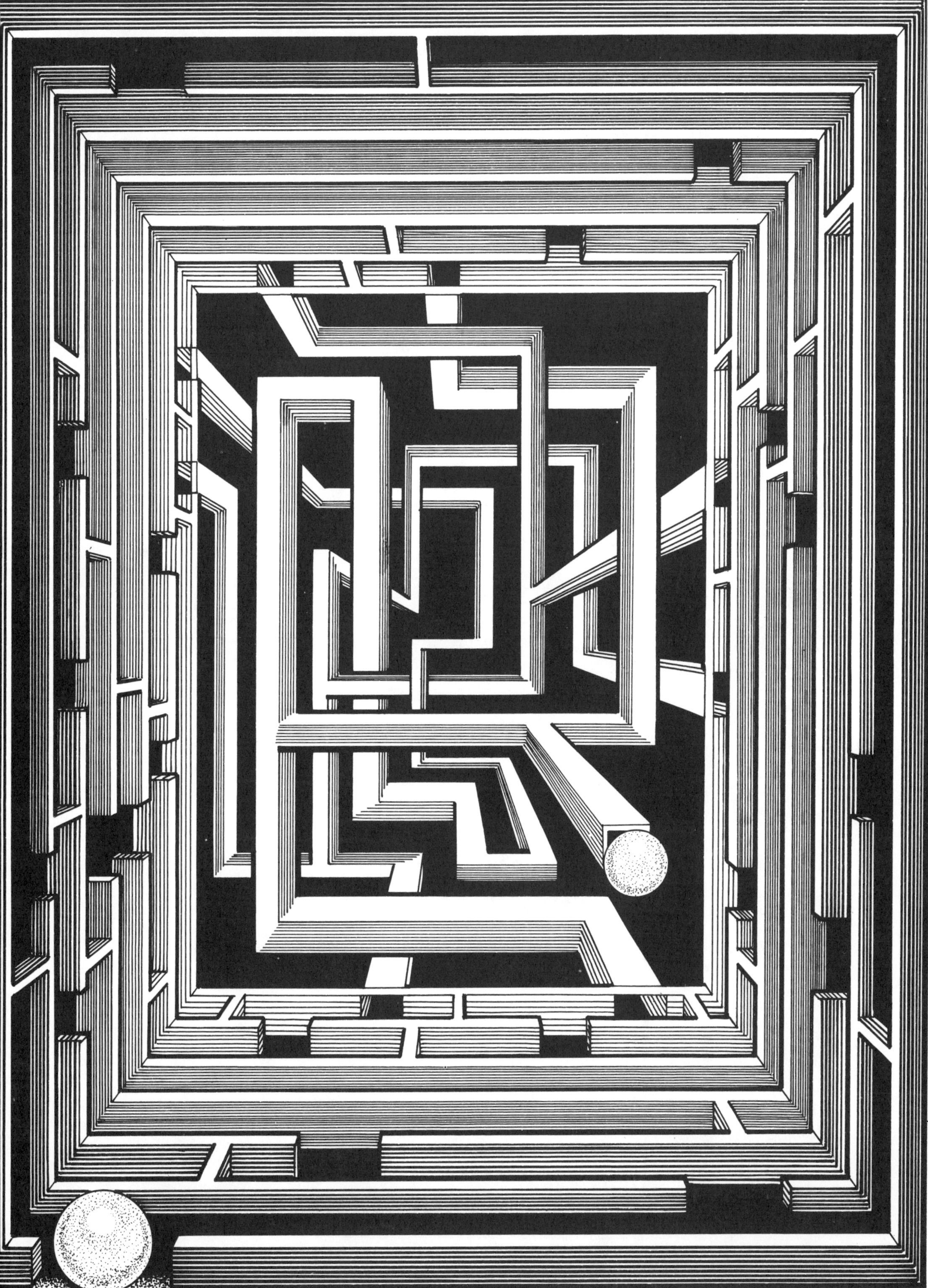

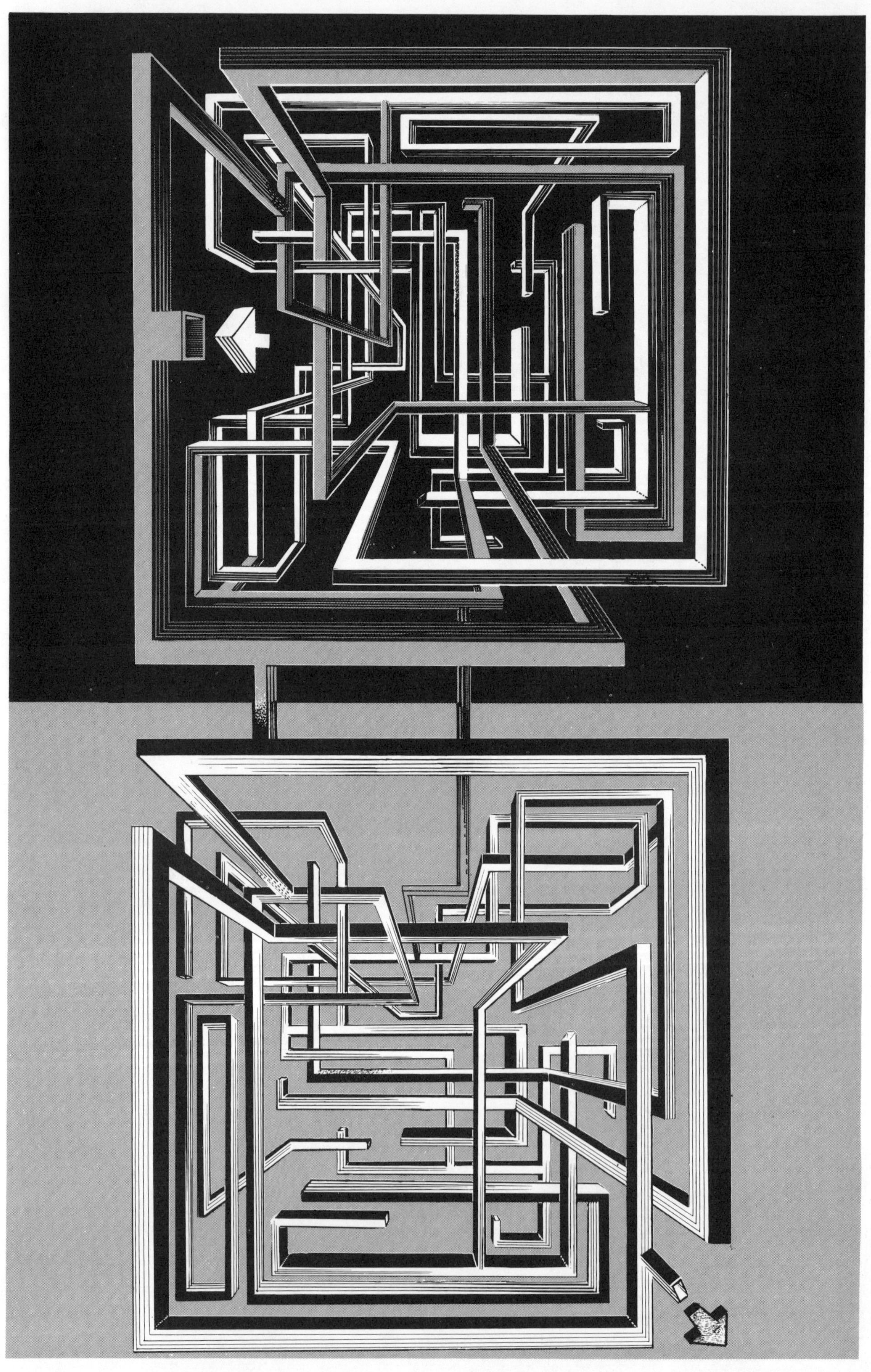

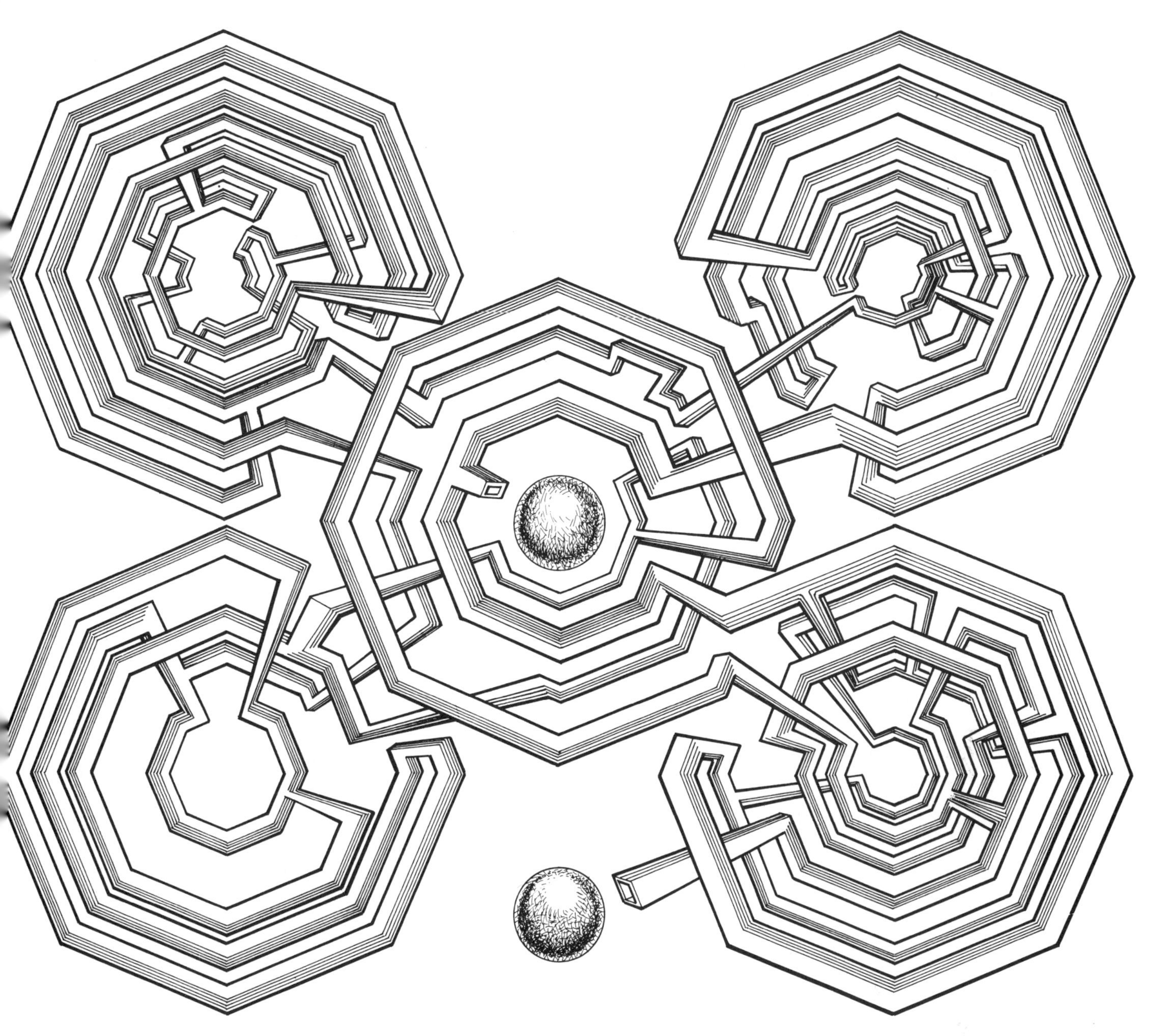

Octahedra Maze
Five polygons contain the tube structure for this maze. The quest is to glide the ball that lies outside the construction through the tubes to the inner globe. This maze contains no dead ends, so if you circle about long enough you're bound to solve it.

Two for One *(p. 34)*
The mechanical engineers tried to save money by duplicating the ducts in these two projects. See if you can find where the air has to go to get from intake to exhaust.

Maurice Escher has said, "I found myself more comfortable in the company of mathematicians than with fellow artists." I find it very difficult to spend much time with anyone (except my wife) over the age of twelve. Children see through all this nonsense we call adulthood pretty quickly. From the little girl who saw no reason to have me autograph her book because my name was already on it, to my entire Little League baseball team (lost thirteen games in a row and soundly humbled their manager), children bring you to your senses. They *always* ask pertinent questions and a child will explore a maze without any hesitation. Adults often find three-dimensional mazes difficult to comprehend. They ask, "Can I go here? Does this path go under here?" or, more often, "This doesn't *even* look like a maze to me!" Children don't do that to you. Usually, seconds after viewing the most devilish construction, a child of six will look up and say, "Don't you have any hard ones?" The mathematicians have discovered three-dimensional mazes also, but, unlike Escher, I think I'll stick to the kids.

The Rose and the Butterfly *(p. 37)*
50cm x 76cm, acrylic on paper.
A circular tube was selected for this maze with a highly reflective surface. The literal-minded tell me that the butterfly is too large to fit into the tube. The answer to that, of course, is to turn metamorphosis into reverse, and have a caterpillar crawl through the pipes to the rose. Notice the difference between this maze and Sky Pipes *on p. 19. Both puzzles use circular tubes, but the different color schemes and backgrounds evoke an entirely different mood.*

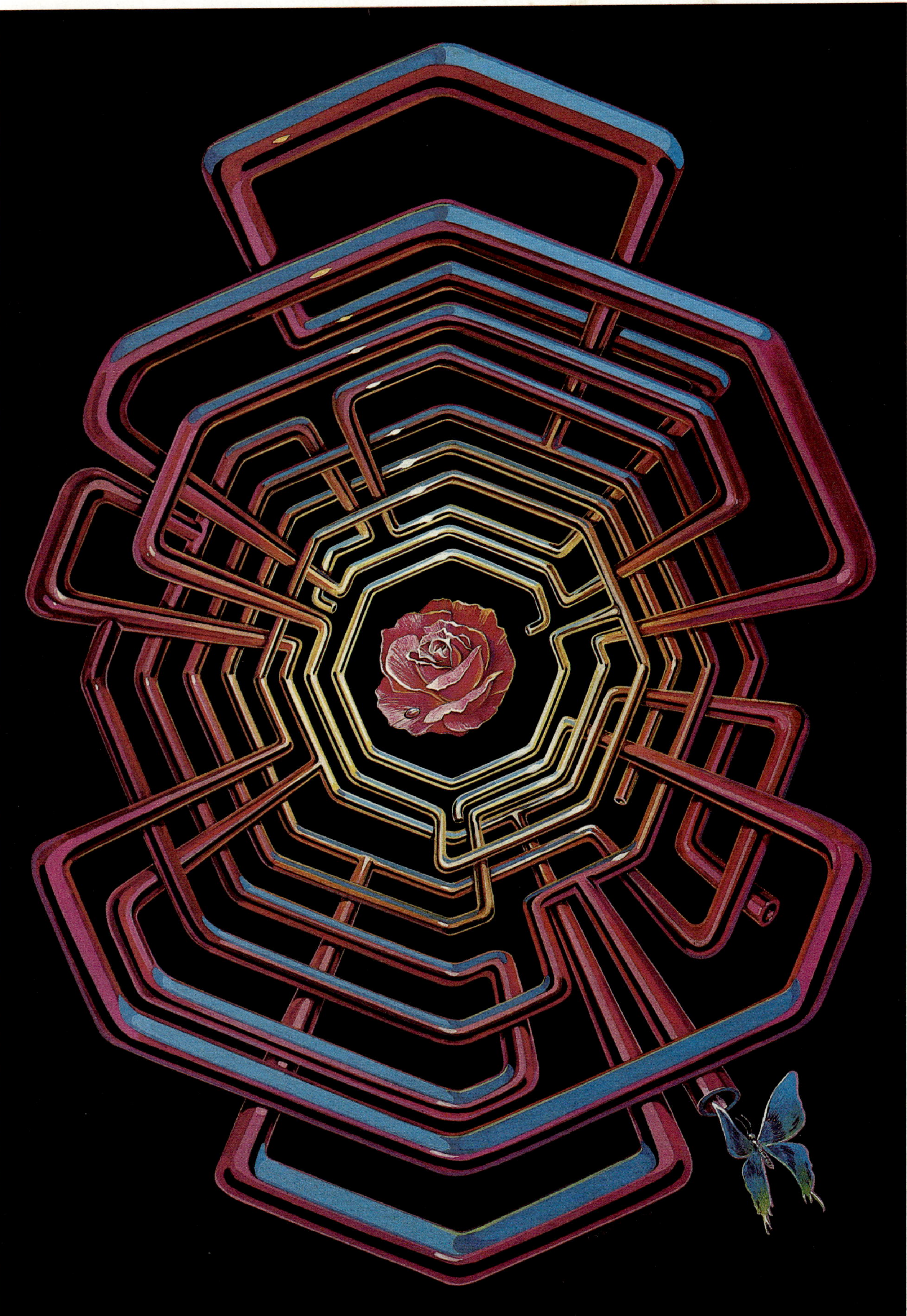

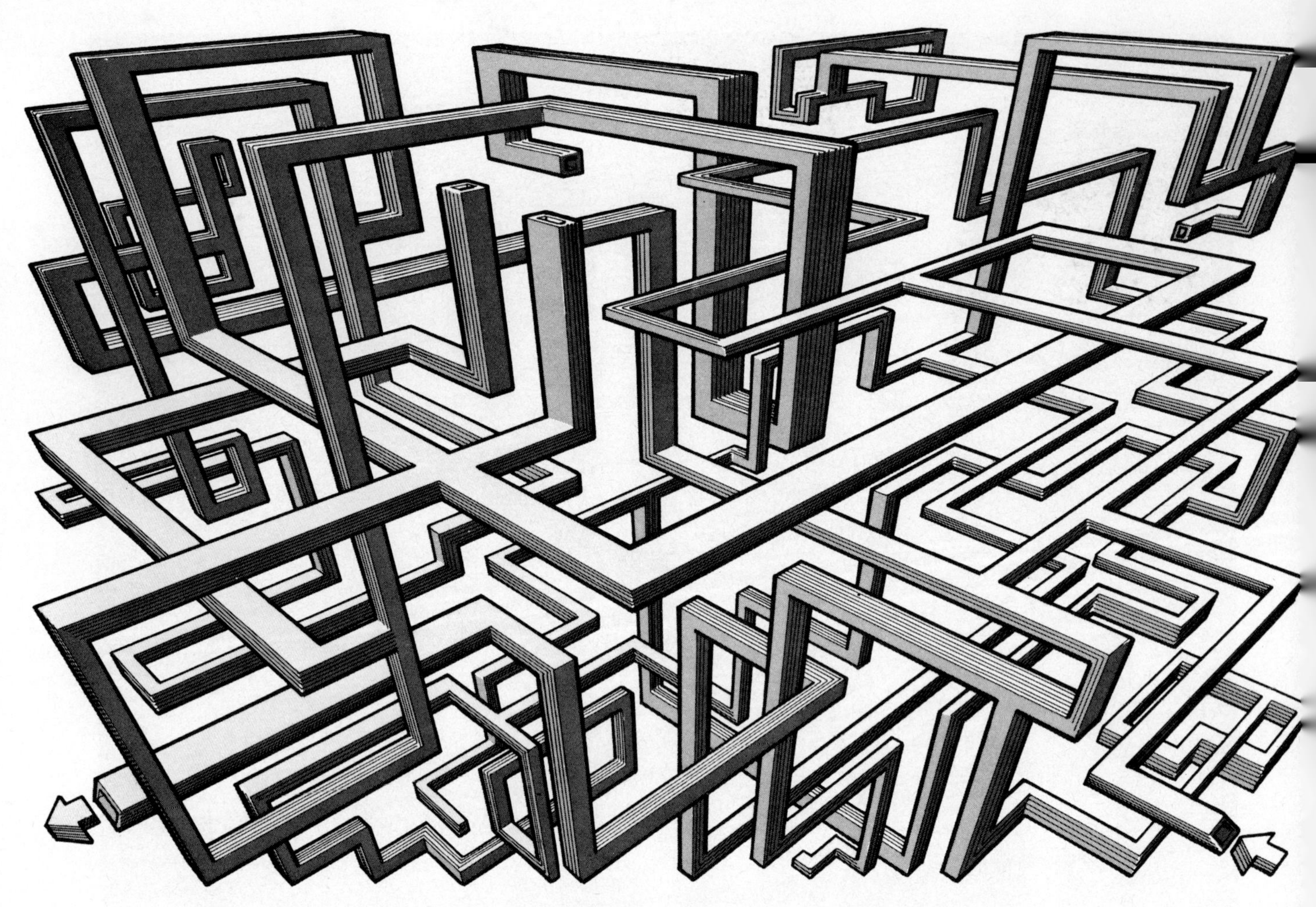

Hydraulics
Obviously, fuel pumped into this system will flow directly from arrow to arrow. Of course, if some spills from an open end, the price will double.

***Cube Root** (p. 39)*
76cm x 100cm, acrylic on canvas.
An homage to Vasarely, this maze asks you to travel through the tubes to connect the four globes to each other. As you travel through the inner cube, see if you can make it reverse from a cut-out area to a free floating cube. The paintings of Vasarely have been a great source of ideas for the mazes. His simplification of shapes and brilliant use of color as well as the use of perspective to create illusions complement the three-dimensional maze concept.

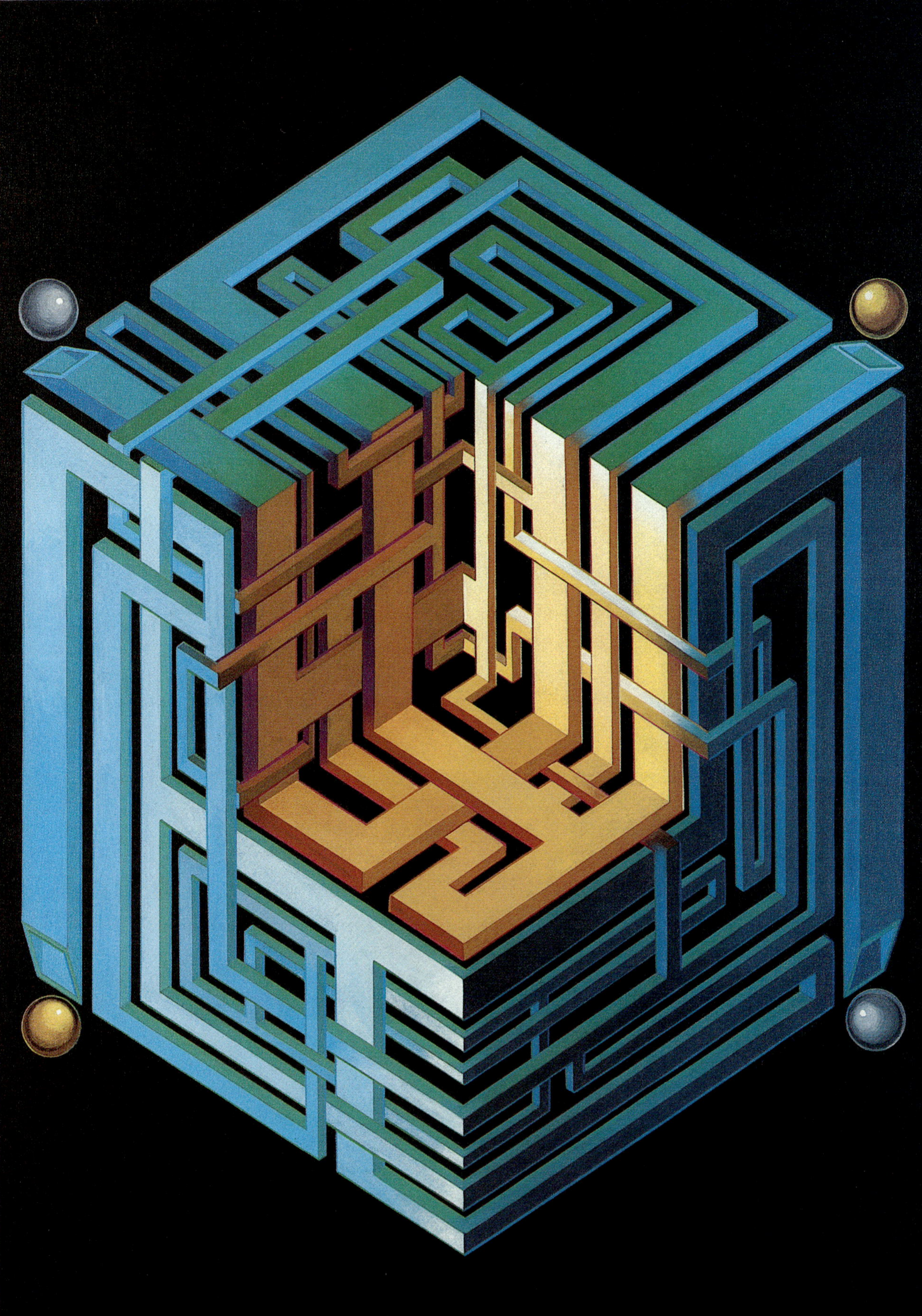

Mazes and other puzzles require a certain kind of logical thinking. A little story I overheard at dinner nicely illustrates just what I mean.

A man was driving his car down the freeway. In the back seat were 21 penguins all bobbing up and down. Suddenly, the car lurched and the man pulled over to the side of the road. He got out to discover he had a flat tire. This was terrible news because he had no spare. He was lucky enough to flag a passing motorist and when the car stopped next to his, he quickly inquired of the occupant, "Could you please help me? I'm taking these 21 penguins to the zoo. My tire is flat and I have no spare. Could you please take these 21 penguins to the zoo for me?"

The man in the other car said, "Sure, I'd be more than glad to."

A transfer was then made and the 21 bouncing penguins were ushered from the back seat of the disabled vehicle to the back seat of the second car. As the kind samaritan's car took off down the road all that could be seen was the 21 penguins, bobbing up and down in the back seat.

The very next day after his tire had been fixed, the first man was driving through town and stopped at a traffic signal. Much to his amazement, the good samaritan's car was stopped right next to his own. In the back seat were the 21 penguins, bobbing up and down.

"I thought I asked you to take those penguins to the zoo," the man called out in some distress.

"I did," came the reply, "and we had such a good time that today we're going to a baseball game."

This little story attempts to mislead you much like a maze does. The obvious connection between the penguins and the zoo leads you in one direction while the story goes in an entirely different one. The number 21 merely adds confusion and it really has nothing to do with the punchline. My three-dimensional mazes also entice you to take the obvious pathway which is usually the wrong way.

Q-Curls *(p. 41)*
50cm x 76cm, acrylic on paper.
Painted electric blue on a red background, the juxtaposition of colors makes the tubes shimmer and float above the surface of the painting.

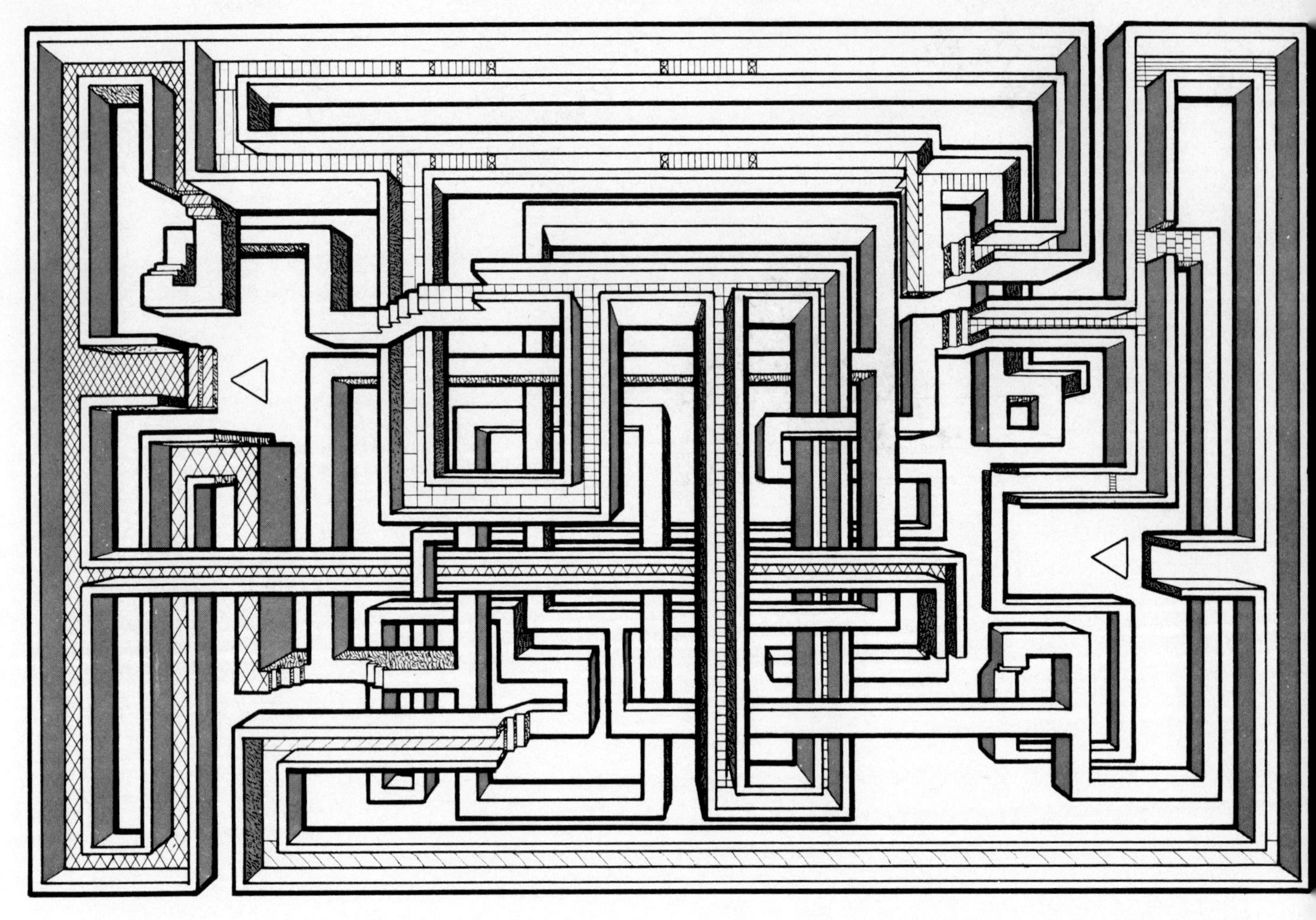

The Plaza
Follow the tile patterns from arrow to arrow without taking any wrong turns. Each time you get lost, start at the other end and try again.

Maze St. Helens *(p. 43)*
50cm x 76cm Acrylic on canvas
During the building of this book, Mt. St. Helens in Washington state blew her top. This maze assumes a view from the inside of the volcano looking up 18 kilometers into the atmosphere. The gold bricks mark the beginning and end of this volcanic labyrinth.

Larry Evans

Chapter 5

Just For the Fun of It

In the previous chapter, you were treated to a series of highly structured compositions that were created to be artistic designs as well as exciting puzzles.

An artist often restricts himself by setting work standards that leave no room for experimentation. Many a fine artist has made a special point of creating humorous drawings and nonsensical art. Picasso often enjoyed producing this kind of work, and it became a large portion of his total repertoire.

The mazes in this chapter were never meant to be fine art, or serious. They are experiments, random ideas that explore labyrinthian concepts beyond the artist's self-imposed rules.

These mazes follow a more whimsical set of rules than those in preceding chapters. Although still based on strict rules of perspective and composition, the themes are more obvious and the mazes less controlled. These compositions are an important part of the experimentation process. Breakthroughs in the development of the mazes happen in the less structured drawings more often than in the highly developed paintings. Whimsical mazes are often better puzzles than the more formal mazes.

It might seem logical, then, to combine the best of the less structured mazes with the best of the serious compositions to create the perfect three-dimensional mazes. Of course, that isn't what happens at all. Each three-dimensional maze has its own identity, and attempting to blend opposite and contrasting ideas within one painting does not guarantee a better result.

At this point, the words "better puzzles" take on a subjective meaning. As the artistic aspects of the maze cannot be separated from the puzzle aspects, the combination of the two elements becomes critical. The maze may not be complex or particularly difficult, but the color or composition may make the picture as a whole more interesting and exciting, and thus a "better puzzle."

The Hardest Maze In The Universe
If you ever wish to be a maze designer, eventually you will have to create your own Hardest Maze in the Universe (p. 44). Using the elements found within mazes in the preceding chapter, The Rose, p. 37 and The Faucet, p. 19, this monstrous composition defies any attempt at solution without Theseus' ball of thread to guide your steps.

The Freeway
As the bridge levels stack one upon the other, the roadway all but disappears. Dashed lines and arrows had to be painted on the road in some places to help guide you through.

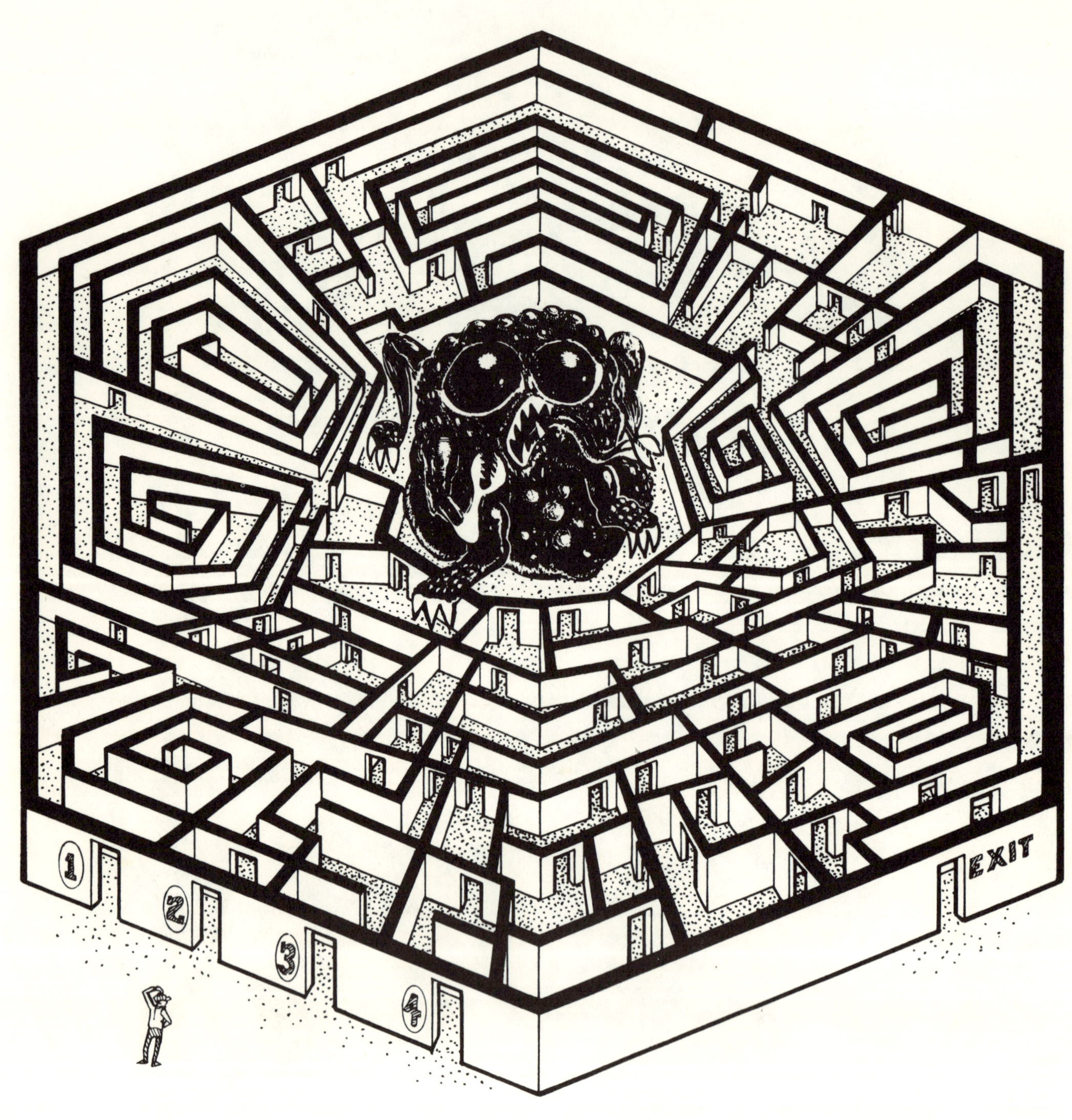

Thesaurus Rex
First published in 3-DIMENSIONAL MONSTER MAZES
(Troubador Press, 1976).
Four doors lead to the labyrinth of the dread monster of the Isle of Synonyms. Find the correct door to lead you to safety. Good luck, best wishes or happy hunting.

Aqueduck

First published in 3-DIMENSIONAL MAZES VOLUME II (Troubador Press, 1977).

Follow the water through the aqueduct as it pours from channel to channel. Flow from the urn to the swimming duck. Note: If you try to work backwards, be careful. *The water flows* down only.

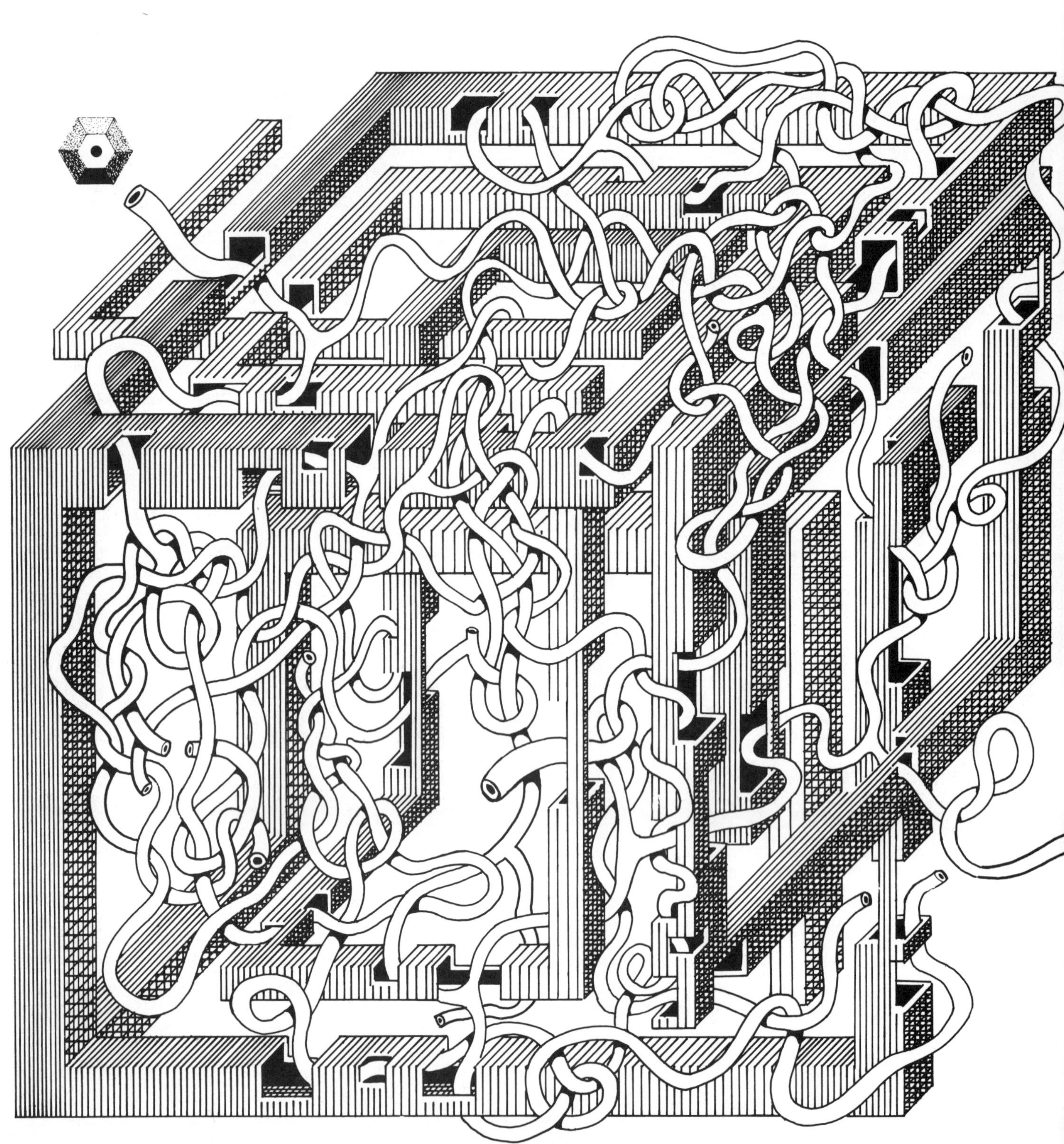

Plasma

Trapped in an octopole magnetic field, the plasma must move quickly through the proton accelerator without escaping. You (and the plasma) are only blocked at the end of a path.

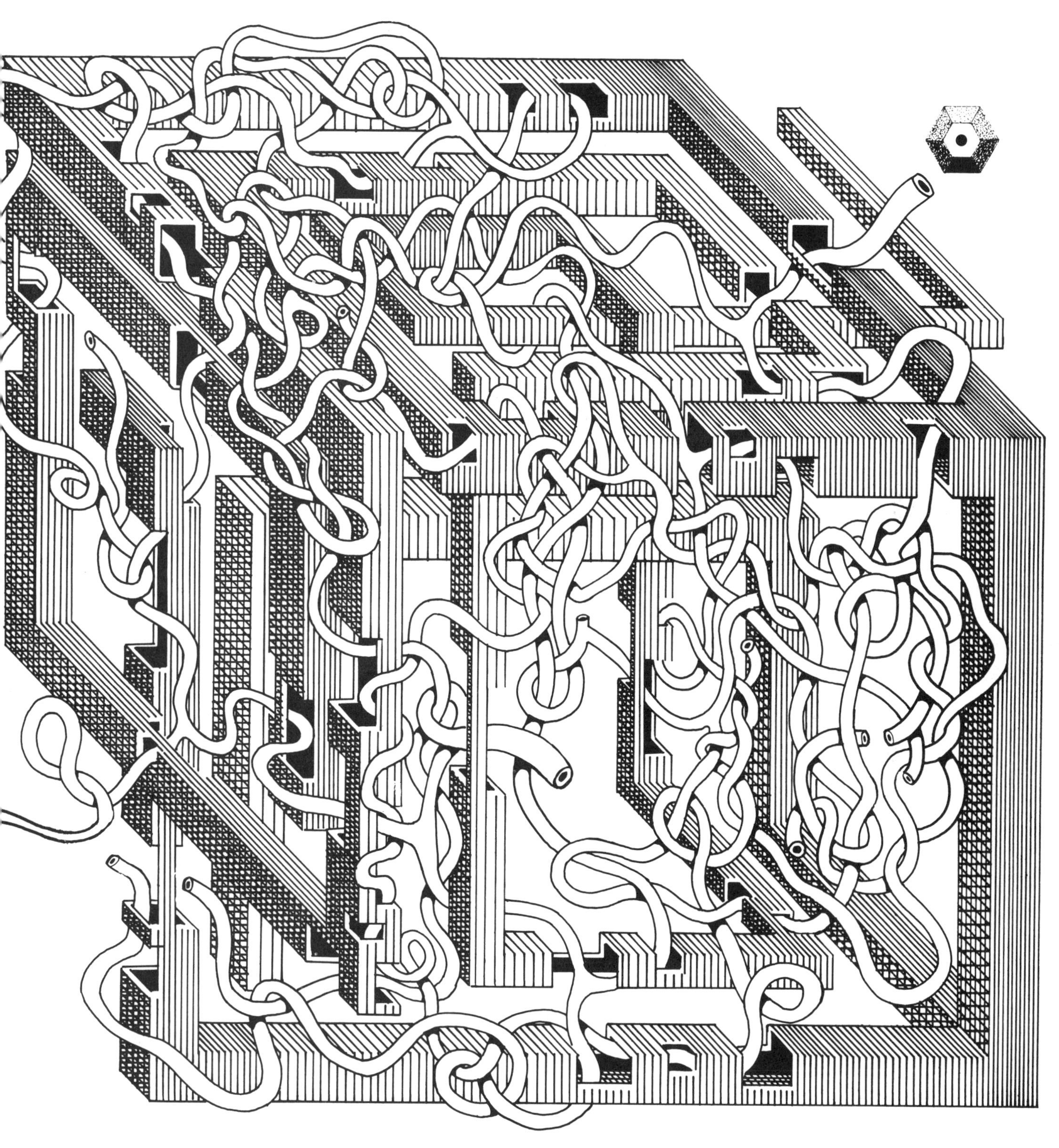

The Reactor
The hydrogen bubble has to pass through the pipes into the reactor core and out again without spilling from an open pipe. By the way, it's thirty seconds to meltdown.

Zig-zag *(p. 53)*
The random tubes weave in and out creating havoc. All the rules of perspective have been thrown out in this explosion.

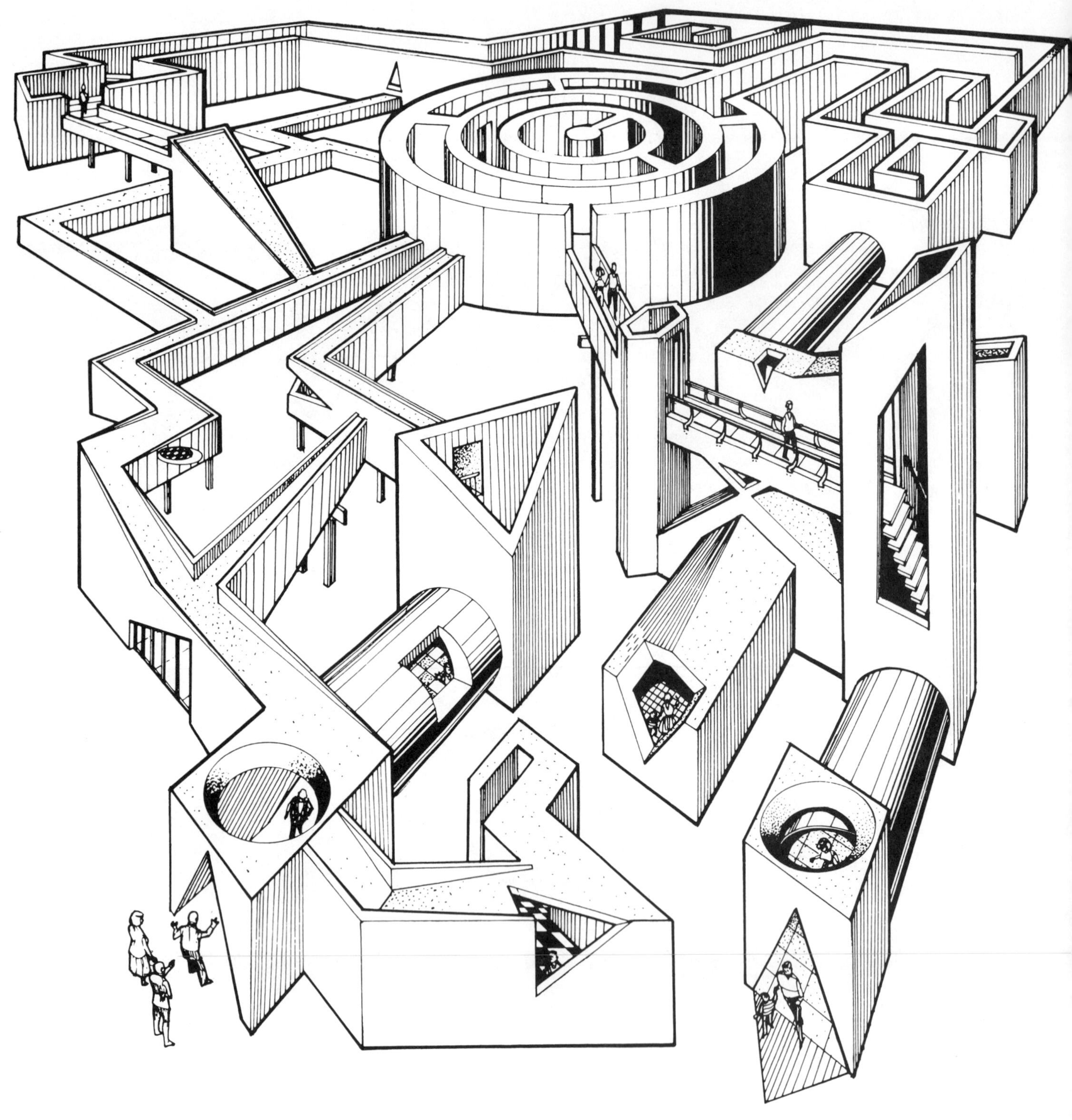

The ultimate three-dimensional maze with audience participation. A variety of textures and shapes greet the intrepid explorer. Optical illusions transform a simple passageway into a nerve wracking experience. Maps are available in "clue boxes" so that nobody will actually get lost. A close-up of the interior environment is on page 59.

Chapter 6

Future Projects — The Three-Dimensional Maze Environment

The natural extension of labyrinthian development is to proceed directly back to its origins. Daedalus had unlimited space to advance his ideas. Imagine a three-dimensional maze so large that one could only experience the labyrinth from within. Our major cities come close to filling the requirements for this type of puzzle, and with very few improvements, I believe a very nice maze could be created out of Detroit or Baltimore (pp. 56 and 57).

On a smaller scale, an environment could be fashioned that might be transportable. It even could have a variety of possible solutions. The experience within the labyrinth would be heightened by the use of optical illusions and unusual textures. The old fashioned sideshow maze that used mirrors as the confounding element is a good example of the impact of just one kind of visual texture. It created incredible tensions with its illusion of inifinite space. The maze itself was often quite simple but the impact was staggering.

With the maze environment that I have in mind, one should take a picnic lunch along because it's going to be quite a while before an exit is achieved. Panic buttons will be installed at major intersections and a team of experienced spelunkers will be on call for major extrications.

The Maze Club

In a society that is growth-oriented, the only possible direction the maze phenomenon can take is the development of the Labyrinthian Club. A membership roster is assembled, a board of directors must be selected and a newsletter printed. Field trips to view mazes will be undertaken. Professors schooled in such matters will be asked to extrapolate the religious aspects of mazes and related puzzles. Exhibit halls should be established in all major urban areas and a traveling exhibit created for those unlucky enough to live in the country. A secret handshake would introduce one member to another, and a variety of maze-related items would be sold through the newsletter. One benefit of the club could be a discount on maps.

City of Tomorrow
First published as CITY OF TOMORROW POSTERBOOK
(Troubador Press, 1978)
Beginning at the train terminal (lower left, p. 57), set your travel plans to arrive at City Hall (upper left, p. 56, with flag). All cities will look like this some day.

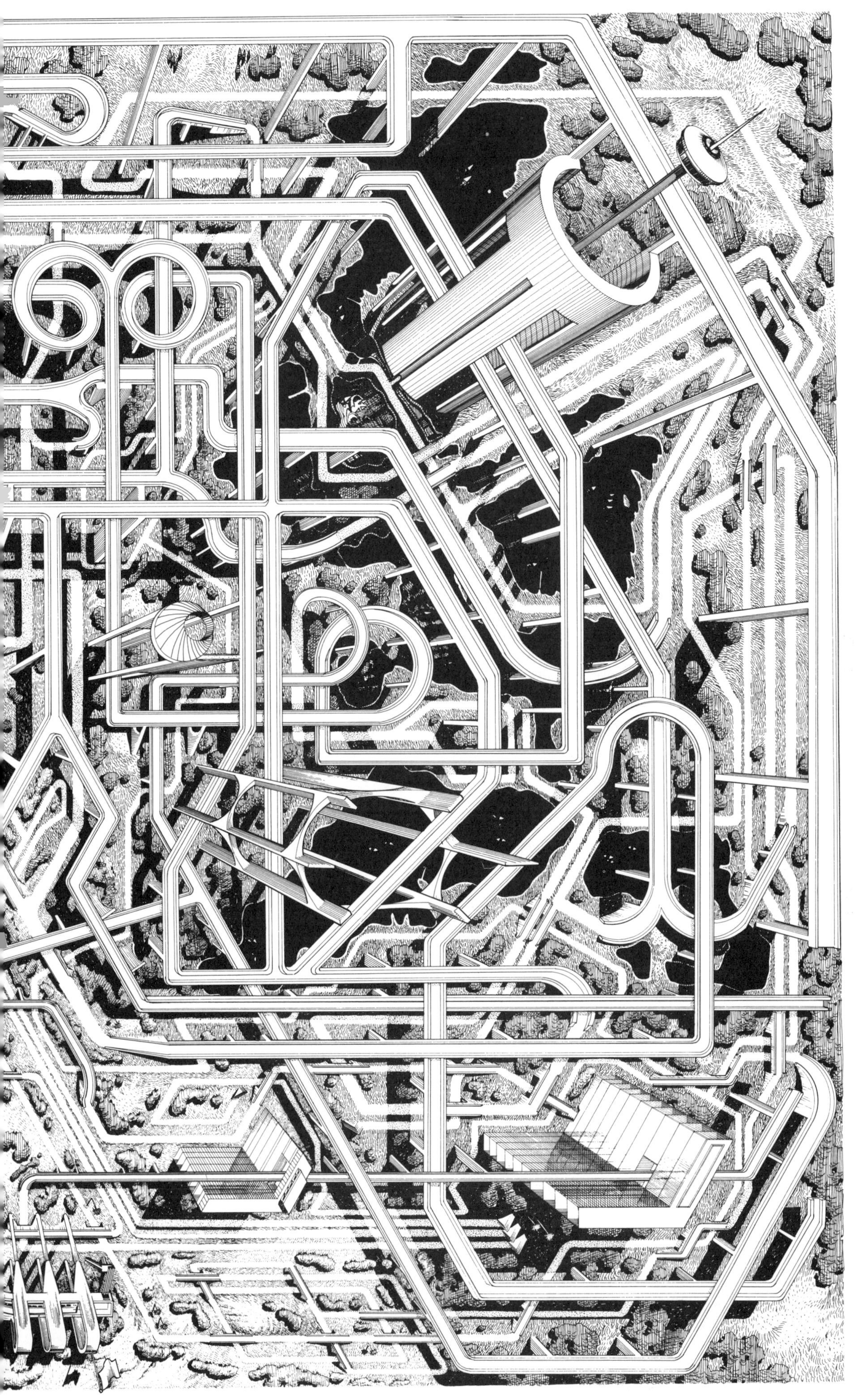

The Final Words on the Subject

In spite of my generally cynical attitude, I tend to take my work seriously. Although no study has ever been made that actually *proves* that life is serious, some aspects of creative work tend to hover on the edge. Art has an important place in everyone's life. If you don't believe me, just try to imagine life without art. Everything you use or touch that has been manufactured had its beginning as a creative idea. Originally, drawings had to be made to design your toothbrush: Sketches and design conferences were required to complete your television set. All of this, before even mentioning the actual painting and sculpture that surrounds us.

The three-dimensional mazes as works of art communicate beyond the limits of painting or drawing. They bring to both the artist and viewer a history of mankind itself. A glimpse into our distant past and possibly into our future. The maze is one of man's oldest symbols. But, it is obviously more than just a symbol. The maze is a pattern of our lives. We can challenge the meandering pathways and force our way through. We can timidly trace our route, leaving a trail of thread to retrace our steps, or choose not to play at all. However the maze is approached, an insight into our innermost selves is exposed by the way we meet the challenge. Perhaps this is why the ancients were so involved with labyrinths. Whatever the reason may have been, the maze has met the test of time and remains one of the strongest graphic symbols known.

The sketch on page 59 illustrates an interior view on the maze environment shown on page 54. Average time taken to traverse this labyrinth is four hours. It is recommended that you pack a picnic lunch and make a day of it.

SOLUTIONS

Page 10

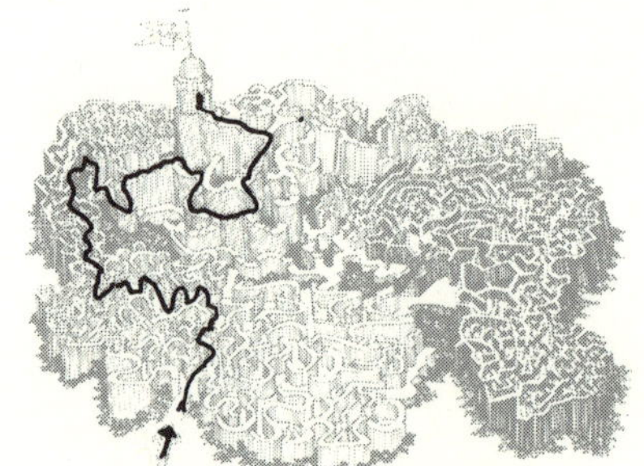
Page 11

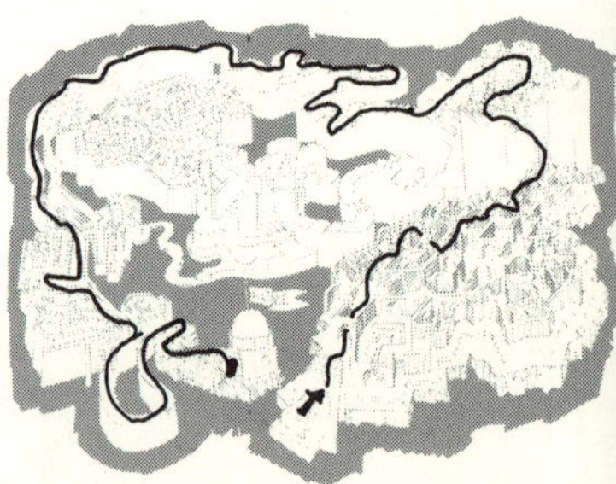
Page 12

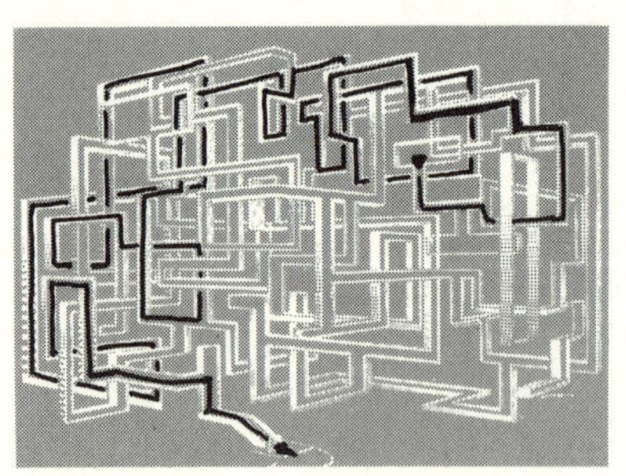
Page 13

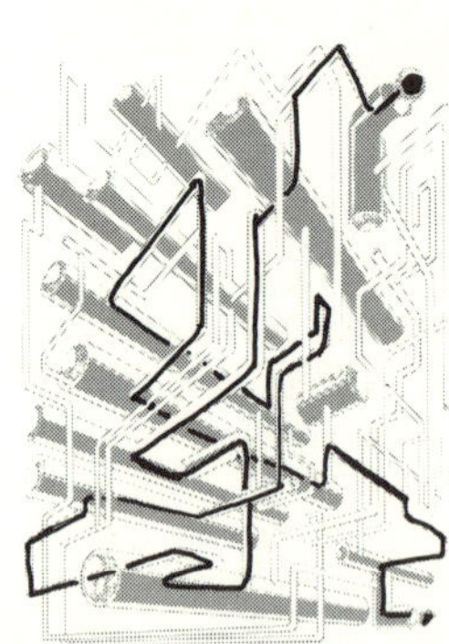
Page 16

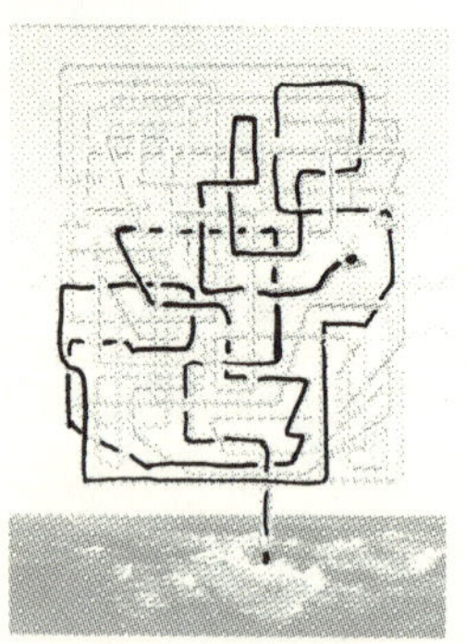
Page 19

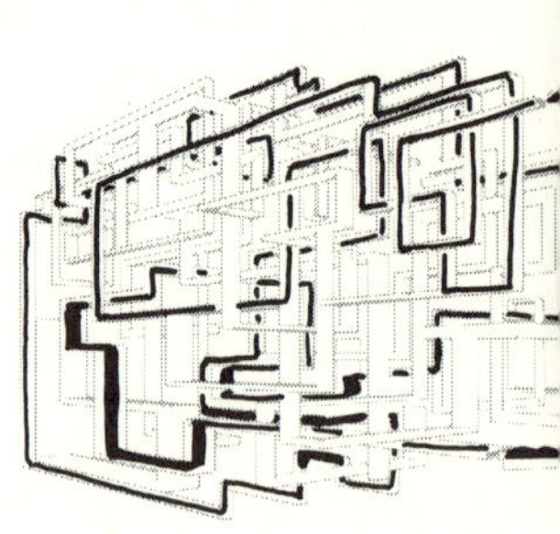
Page 20

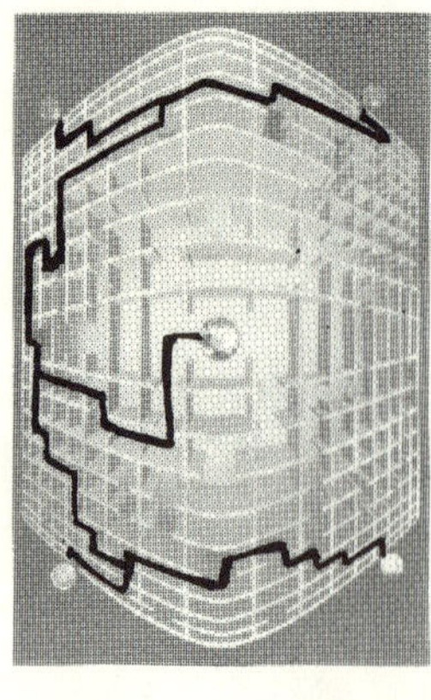
Page 21

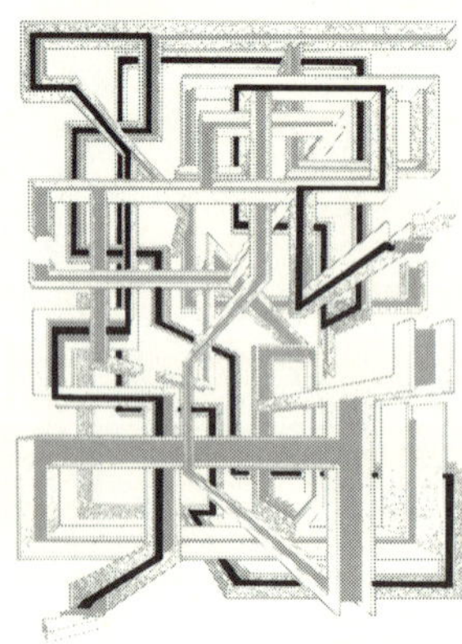
Page 22

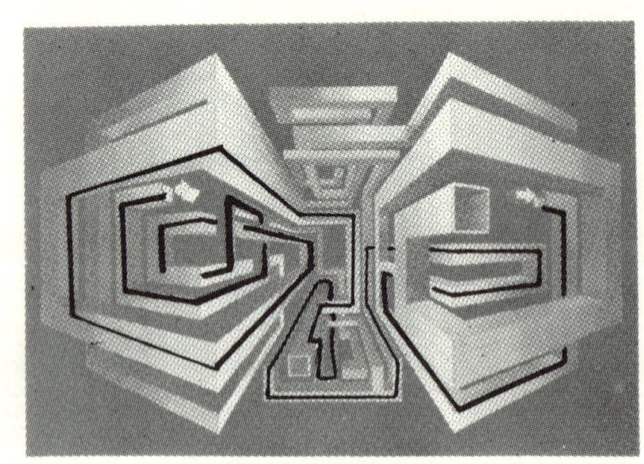
Page 23 (top)

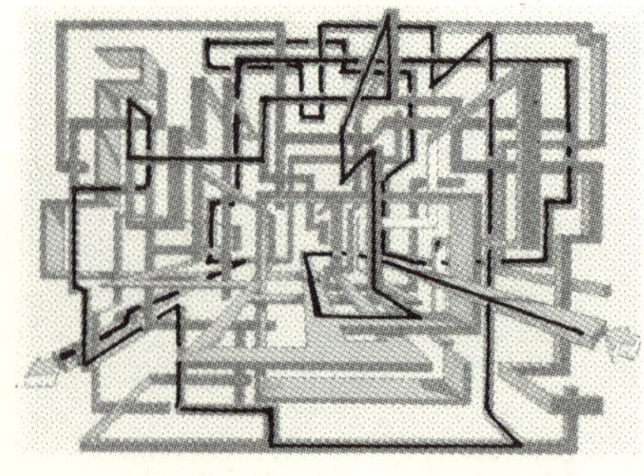
Page 23 (bottom)

Page 25

Page 26

SOLUTIONS

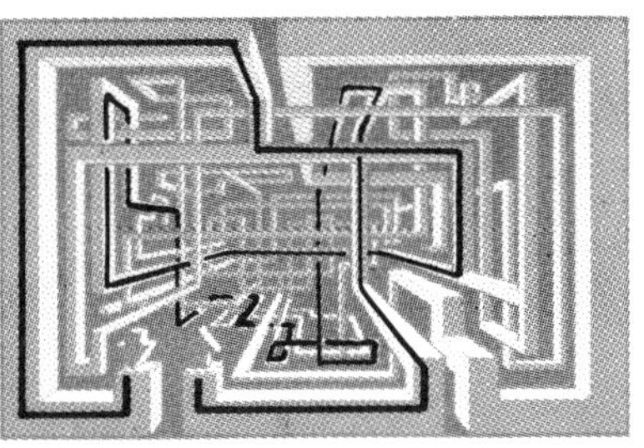

Page 27

Page 28

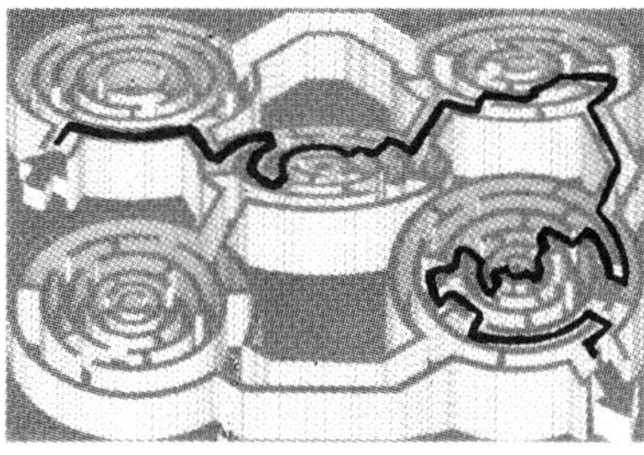

Page 29

Page 30

Page 31

Page 33

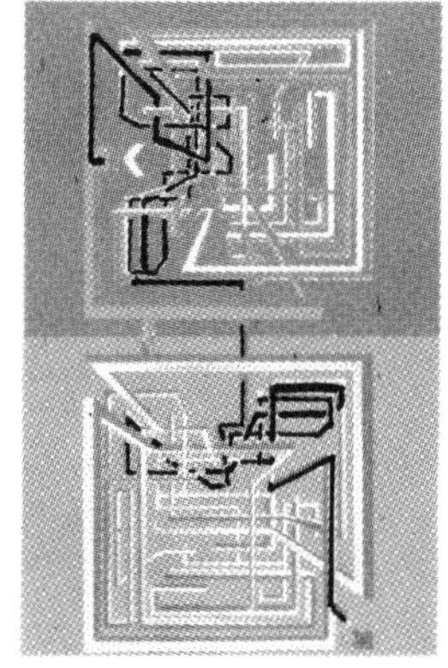

Page 34

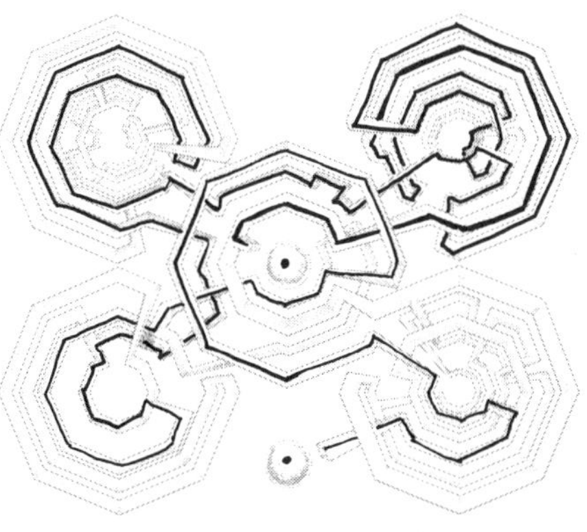

Page 35

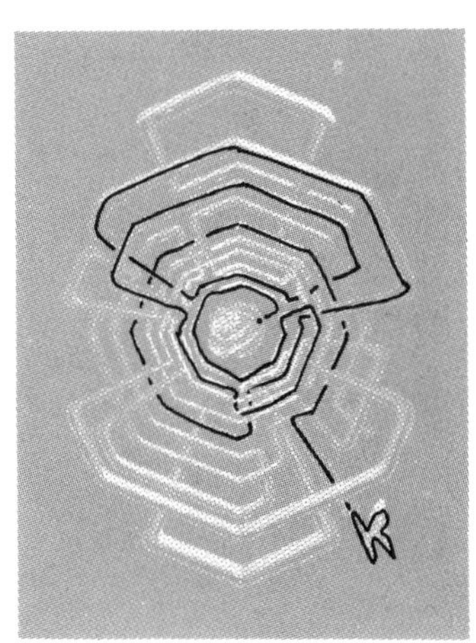

Page 37

SOLUTIONS

Page 38

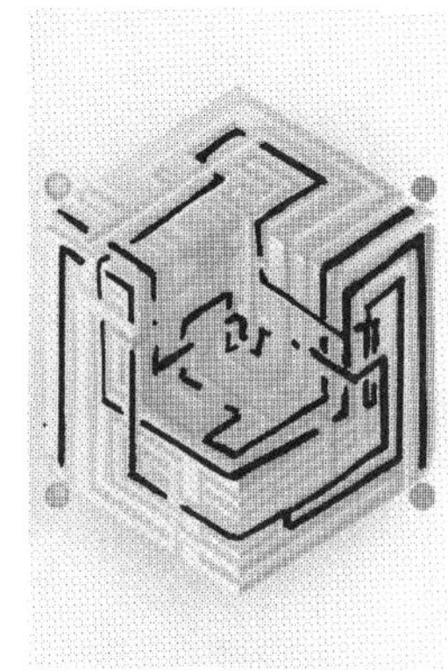

Page 39

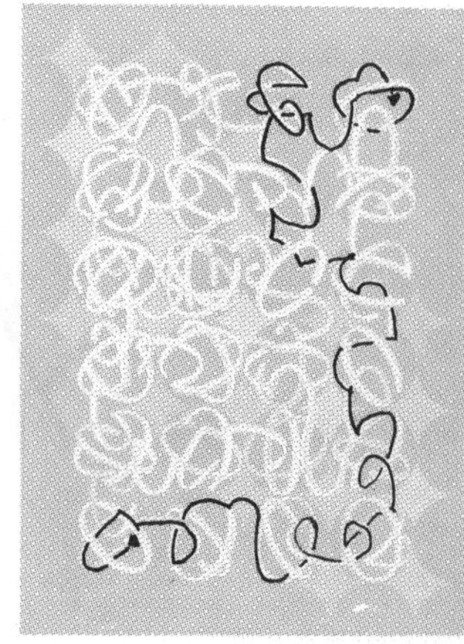

Page 41

Page 42

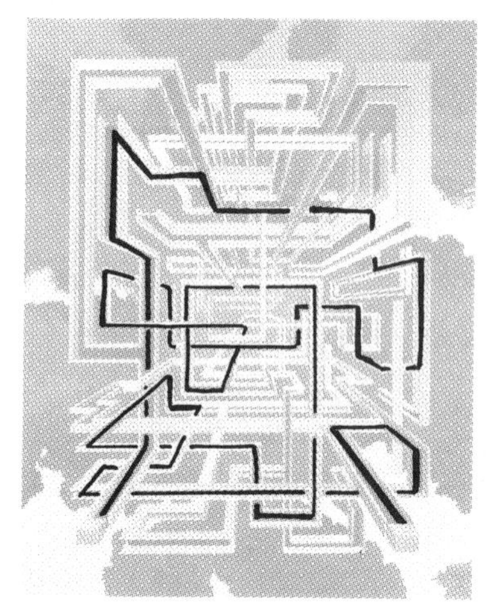

Page 43

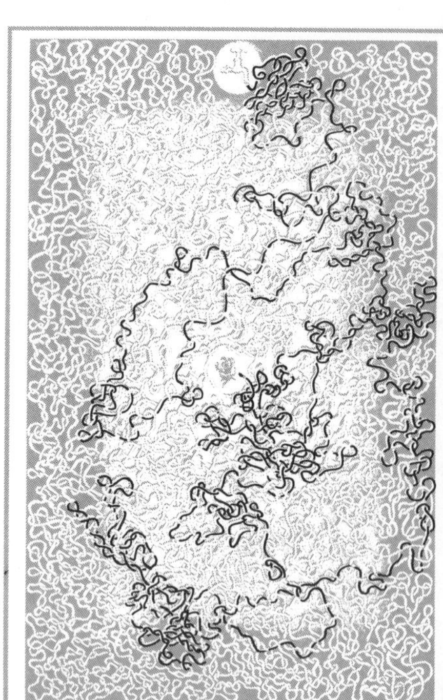

Page 44

Pages 46-47

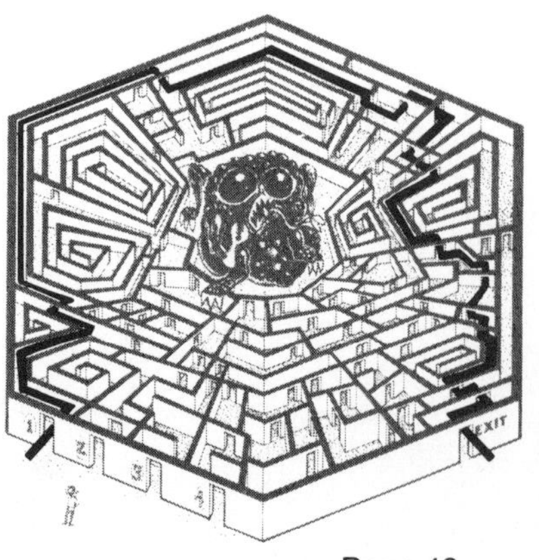

Page 48

SOLUTIONS

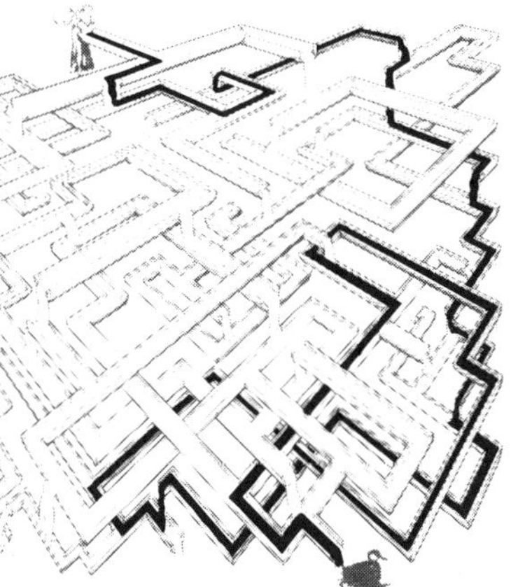

Page 49

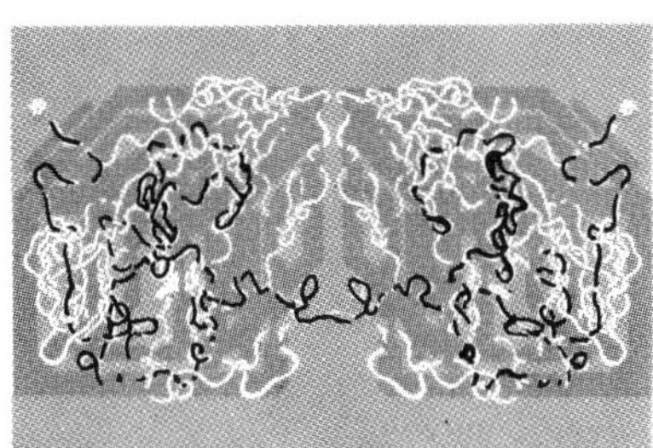

Pages 50-51

Page 52

Page 53

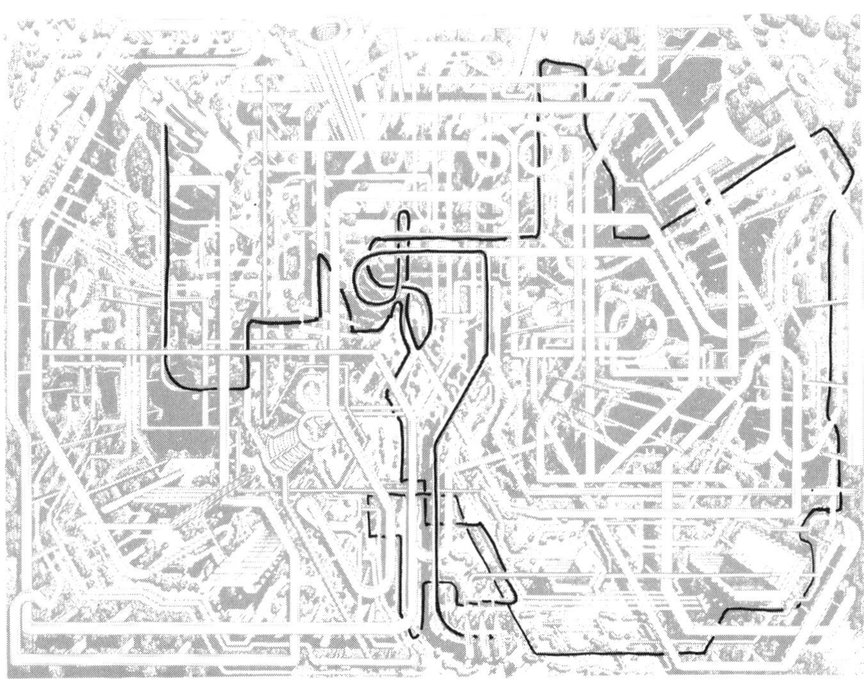

Pages 56-57

FRONT COVER

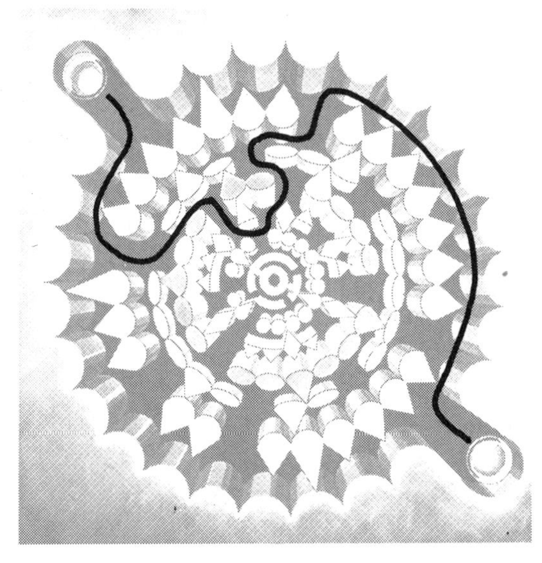

BACK COVER

MORE TROUBADOR BOOKS BY LARRY EVANS

3-Dimensional Mazes
3-Dimensional Mazes Vol. 2
3-Dimensional Monster Mazes
Space Maze Posterbook
City of Tomorrow Posterbook
Fantastic Journey Posterbook
Pyramid Puzzles
Victorian Puzzles
Gorey Games
3-Dimensional Optical Illusions
Space WARP Color and Story Album
How to Draw Monsters
How to Draw Prehistoric Monsters
How to Draw Robots and Spaceships
InVisibles
Gnomes Games